who was Wanted

by SIR ARTHUR CONAN DOYLE

The most famous detective of all time solves his last case!

A recently discovered and heretofore unpublished

novelette starring the immortal Sherlock Holmes

During the late autumn of 'ninety-five a fortunate chance enabled me to take some part in another of my friend Sherlock Holmes's fascinating cases.

My wife not having been well for some time, I had at last persuaded her to take a holiday in Switzerland in the company of her old school friend Kate Whitney, whose name may be remembered in connection with the strange case I have already chronicled under the title of "The Man with the Twisted Lip." My practice had grown much, and I had been working very hard for many months and never felt in more need myself of a rest and a holiday. Unfortunately I dared not absent myself for a long enough period to warrant a visit to the Alps. I promised my wife, however, that I would get a week or ten days' holiday in somehow, and it was only on this understanding that she consented to the Swiss tour I was so anxious for her to take. One of my best patients was in a very critical state at the time, and it was not until August was gone that he passed the crisis and began to recover. Feeling then that I could leave my practice with a good conscience in the hands of a *locum tenens*, I began to wonder where and how I should best find the rest and change I needed.

Almost at once the idea came to my mind that I would hunt up my old friend Sherlock Holmes, of whom I had seen nothing for several months. If he had no important inquiry in hand, I would do my uttermost to persuade him to join me.

Within half an hour of coming to this resolution I was standing in the doorway of the familiar old room in Baker Street.

Holmes was stretched upon the couch with his back towards me, the familiar dressing gown and old brier pipe as much in evidence as of yore.

"Come in, Watson," he cried, without glancing round. "Come in and tell me what good wind blows you here?"

Published by Arrangement with the Estate of the Late Sir Arthur Conan Doyle
Copyright, 1948, by Denis P. S. Conan Doyle, Executor of the Estate of the late Sir Arthur Conan Doyle

NOVA 57 MINOR

The endpaper and title-page drawings are by Robert Fawcett, an important American book and magazine illustrator in the 1940s and '50s. Ironically, he would also illustrate all but one of the twelve *Exploits of Sherlock Holmes* written by Adrian Conan Doyle and the famous mystery author John Dickson Carr, when they first appeared in *Collier's* in 1953. (Courtesy of Hearst Publications)

JON L. LELLENBERG

NOVA *57* MINOR

THE WAXING AND WANING OF
THE SIXTY-FIRST ADVENTURE OF
SHERLOCK HOLMES

TOGETHER WITH
THAT "SIXTY-FIRST ADVENTURE"
THE MAN WHO WAS WANTED
BY ARTHUR WHITAKER

for Bill Hyder,
with warm Irregular wishes
from Jon Lellenberg
Jan. 10, 1998

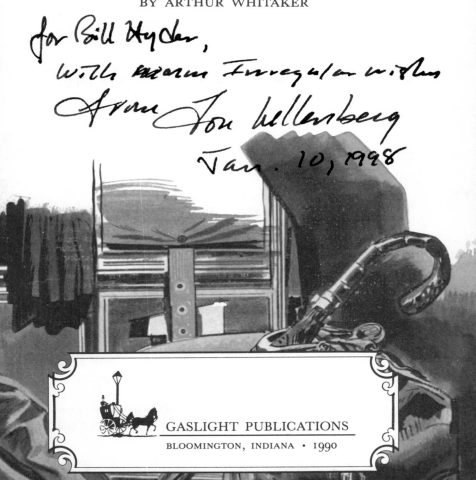

GASLIGHT PUBLICATIONS
BLOOMINGTON, INDIANA · 1990

To the Baker Street Irregulars —
especially the Doyleans among us

———

The endpaper and title-page illustrations by Robert Fawcett are reprinted with permission from *Cosmopolitan Magazine,* August 1948. *Cosmopolitan* is a publication of Hearst Magazines, a division of The Hearst Corporation. Copyright © 1948 by The Hearst Corporation.

ISBN: 0-934468-26-5

Library of Congress
Catalogue Card No. 89-80834

First Edition: February 1990
Printed in the United States of America

GASLIGHT PUBLICATIONS
626 North College Avenue
Bloomington, Indiana 47404

Contents

NOVA 57 MINOR

FOREWORD

ADRIAN CONAN DOYLE called it "this absurd affair of
Whitaker and the Holmes Story That Wasn't." Edgar W.
Smith thought it either a deliberate hoax by the Conan
Doyle Estate or else "a mark of the incredible stupidity
which has marked so many of their actions." Vincent
Starrett was mainly concerned that Sir Arthur Conan
Doyle's reputation come out of it well. What was it? It was
the series of events that led an apocryphal Sherlock Holmes
story called "The Man Who Was Wanted" to be mistakenly
published in both the United States and Great Britain as the
work of Sir Arthur Conan Doyle.

The outlines of the episode should be familiar by now.
The world quite comfortably believed that the four novels
and fifty-six short stories published in *The Complete Sherlock
Holmes* comprised the entire Sherlockian Canon of sixty
adventures. But, in 1942, the typescript of an unpublished
Sherlock Holmes story was discovered among Sir Arthur
Conan Doyle's papers. Despite statements by his sons Denis
and Adrian that the story was not up to their father's
standard, there was great clamor to have it published; and
no doubt the financial potential of an unpublished Sherlock
Holmes story was not lost upon the Conan Doyle Estate.
In due course, it did appear—only to have its authorship
quickly claimed by an unknown, retired English architect
named Arthur Whitaker (born 1882). Whitaker said that he
had written it in 1910 and sold it for ten guineas to Sir
Arthur, who had declined any collaboration but was willing
to pay for the possible use of the story idea. When this claim

surfaced, the reaction of the Conan Doyle Estate was immediate, direct, and vitriolic. It was also premature: Whitaker was able to prove that the story *was* his work. And so it became known that "The Man Who Was Wanted," instead of being the sixty-first Canonical adventure, was only a pastiche.

But, even more than forty years after the story's publication, one can still find references to "The Man Who Was Wanted" as an unpublished tale by Sir Arthur Conan Doyle. In recent years, critics as learned as Trevor Hall, in *Sherlock Holmes and His Creator* (Duckworth, 1978), and Peter Haining, in *The Final Adventures of Sherlock Holmes* (Castle, 1981), discussed it as a story that Sir Arthur had written and then put aside. And even those who have known better have not known the series of events which took place away from the public view four decades ago: how Whitaker's claim came to light, how it was investigated and established, and the tempers and intemperate words that flew across England and the Atlantic Ocean.

The following account, originally published in briefer form in 1978 as a Dispatch-Box Press monograph (De Waal 4727B), in an edition of only twenty copies, tells of those events, and of the campaign on the part of a number of Baker Street Irregulars (among them Nathan Bengis, Anthony Boucher, Charles Honce, Edgar W. Smith, P. M. Stone, and especially Vincent Starrett) to see the story published, and later to have the truth of its authorship established. Of assistance of me in the research for this work have been a number of other Baker Street Irregulars: the late Bliss Austin, Peter E. Blau, the late Dean Dickinsheet, Michael Harrison, Richard Lancelyn Green, the late Michael Murphy, Donald A. Redmond, and John Bennett Shaw. Michael Murphy and Richard Lancelyn Green were especially helpful in making available important collections of letters in their possession, as was Michael Holroyd, past president of England's Society of Authors. I am grateful to them for permission to quote from those collections, and also to Dame Jean Conan Doyle and Mrs. Anna Conan Doyle for their co-operation.

—J.L.

The Man Who Was Wanted

DURING the late autumn of 'ninety-five a fortunate chance enabled me to take some part in another of my friend Sherlock Holmes's fascinating cases.

My wife not having been well for some time, I had at last persuaded her to take a holiday in Switzerland in the company of her old school friend Kate Whitney, whose name may be remembered in connection with the strange case I have already chronicled under the title of "The Man with the Twisted Lip." My practice had grown much, and I had been working very hard for many months and never felt in more need myself of a rest and a holiday. Unfortunately I dared not absent myself for a long enough period to warrant a visit to the Alps. I promised my wife, however, that I would get a week or ten days' holiday in somehow, and it was only on this understanding that she consented to the Swiss tour I was so anxious for her to take. One of my best patients was in a very critical state at the time, and it was not until August was gone that he passed the crisis and began to recover. Feeling then that I could leave my practice with a good conscience in the hands of a *locum tenens,* I began to wonder where and how I should best find the rest and change I needed.

Almost at once the idea came to my mind that I would hunt up my old friend Sherlock Holmes, of whom I had seen nothing for several months. If he had no important inquiry in hand, I would do my uttermost to persuade him to join me.

Within half an hour of coming to this resolution I was standing in the doorway of the familiar old room in Baker Street.

Holmes was stretched upon the couch with his back towards me, the familiar dressing gown and old brier pipe as much in evidence as of yore.

"Come in, Watson," he cried, without glancing round. "Come in and tell me what good wind blows you here?"

"What an ear you have, Holmes," I said. "I don't think that I could have recognized your tread so easily."

"Nor I yours," said he, "if you hadn't come up my badly lighted staircase taking the steps two at a time with all the familiarity of an old fellow lodger; even then I might not have been sure who it was, but when you stumbled over the new mat outside the door which has been there for nearly three months, you needed no further announcement."

Holmes pulled out two or three of the cushions from the pile he was lying on and threw them across into the armchair. "Sit down, Watson, and make yourself comfortable; you'll find cigarettes in a box behind the clock."

As I proceeded to comply, Holmes glanced whimsically across at me. "I'm afraid I shall have to disappoint you, my boy," he said. "I had a wire only half an hour ago which will prevent me from joining in any little trip you may have been about to propose."

"Really, Holmes," I said, "don't you think this is going a little *too* far? I begin to fear you are a fraud and pretend to discover things by observation, when all the time you really do it by pure out-and-out clairvoyance!"

Holmes chuckled. "Knowing you as I do it's absurdly simple," said he. "Your surgery hours are from five to seven, yet at six o'clock you walk smiling into my rooms. Therefore you must have a *locum* in. You are looking well, though tired, so the obvious reason is that you are having, or about to have, a holiday. The clinical thermometer, peeping out of your pocket, proclaims that you have been on your rounds today, hence it's pretty evident that your real holiday begins tomorrow. When, under these circumstances, you come hurrying into my rooms—which, by the way, Watson, you haven't visited for nearly three months—with a new Bradshaw and a timetable of excursion bookings bulging out of your coat pocket, then it's more than probable you have come with the idea of suggesting some joint expedition."

"It's all perfectly true," I said, and explained to him, in a few words, my plans. "And I'm more disappointed than I can tell you," I concluded, "that you are not able to fall in with my little scheme."

Holmes picked up a telegram from the table and looked at it thoughtfully. "If only the inquiry this refers to promised to be of anything like the interest of some we have gone into together, nothing would have delighted me more than to have persuaded you to throw your lot in with mine for a time; but really I'm afraid to do so, for it sounds a particularly commonplace affair," and he crumpled the paper into a ball and tossed it over to me.

I smoothed it out and read: "To Holmes, 221B Baker Street, London, S.W. Please come to Sheffield at once to inquire into case of forgery. Jervis, Manager British Consolidated Bank."

"I've wired back to say I shall go up to Sheffield by the one-thirty-A.M. express from St. Pancras," said Holmes. "I can't go sooner as I have an interesting little appointment to fulfill tonight down in the East End, which should give me the last information I need to trace home a daring robbery from the British Museum to its instigator—who possesses one of the oldest titles and finest houses in the country, along with a most insatiable greed, almost mania, for collecting ancient documents. Before discussing the Sheffield affair any further, however, we had perhaps better see what the evening paper has to say about it," continued Holmes, as his boy entered with the *Evening News, Standard, Globe,* and *Star.* "Ah, this must be it," he said, pointing to a paragraph headed: "Daring Forger's Remarkable Exploits in Sheffield."

Whilst going to press we have been informed that a series of most cleverly forged cheques have been successfully used to swindle the Sheffield banks out of a sum which cannot be less than six thousand pounds. The full extent of the fraud has not yet been ascertained, and the managers of the different banks concerned, who have been interviewed by our Sheffield correspondent, are very reticent.

It appears that a gentleman named Mr. Jabez Booth, who resides at Broomhill, Sheffield, and has been an employee since January 1881, at the British Consolidated Bank in Sheffield, yesterday succeeded in cashing quite a number of cleverly forged cheques at twelve of the principal banks in the city and absconding with the proceeds.

The crime appears to have been a strikingly deliberate and well-thought-out one. Mr. Booth had, of course, in his position in one of the principal banks in Sheffield, excellent opportunities of studying the various signatures which he forged, and he greatly facilitated his chances of easily and successfully obtaining cash for the cheques by opening banking accounts last year at each of the twelve banks at which he presented the forged cheques, and by this means becoming personally known at each.

He still further disarmed suspicion by crossing each of the forged cheques and paying them into his account, while, at the same time, he drew and cashed a cheque of his own for about half the amount of the forged cheque paid in.

It was not until early this morning, Thursday, that the fraud was discovered, which means that the rascal has had some twenty hours in which to make good his escape. In spite of this we have little doubt but that he will soon be laid by the heels, for we are informed that the finest detectives from Scotland Yard are already upon his track, and it is also whispered that Mr. Sherlock Holmes, the well-known and almost world-famed criminal expert of Baker Street, has been asked to assist in hunting down this daring forger.

"Then there follows a lengthy description of the fellow, which I needn't read but will keep for future use," said Holmes, folding the paper and looking across at me. "It seems to have been a pretty smart affair. This Booth may not be easily caught for, though he hasn't had a long time in which to make his escape, we mustn't lose sight of the fact that he's had twelve months in which to plan how he would do the vanishing trick when the time came. Well! What do you say, Watson? Some of the little problems we have gone into in the past should at least have taught us that the most interesting cases do not always present the most bizarre features at the outset."

" 'So far from it, on the contrary, quite the reverse,' to quote Sam Weller," I replied. "Personally nothing would be more to my taste than to join you."

"Then we'll consider it settled," said my friend. "And now I must go and attend to that other little matter of business I spoke to you about. Remember," he said, as we parted, "one-thirty at St. Pancras."

I was on the platform in good time, but it was not until the hands of the great station clock indicated the very moment due for our departure, and the porters were beginning to slam the carriage doors noisily, that I caught the familiar sight of Holmes's tall figure.

"Ah! here you are, Watson," he cried cheerily. "I fear you must have thought I was going to be too late. I've had a very busy evening and no time to waste; however, I've succeeded in putting into practice Phileas Fogg's theory that 'a well-used minimum suffices for everything,' and here I am."

"About the last thing I should expect of you," I said as we settled down into two opposite corners of an otherwise empty first-class carriage, "would be that you should do such an unmethodical thing as to miss a train. The only thing which would surprise me more, in fact, would be to see you at the station ten minutes before time."

"I should consider that the greatest evil of the two," said Holmes sententiously. "But now we must sleep; we have every prospect of a heavy day."

It was one of Holmes's characteristics that he could command sleep at will; unfortunately he could resist it at will also, and often have I had to remonstrate with him on the harm he must be doing himself, when, deeply engrossed in one of his strange or baffling problems, he would go for several consecutive days and nights without one wink of sleep.

He put the shades over the lamps, leaned back in his corner, and in less than two minutes his regular breathing told me he was fast asleep. Not being blessed with the same gift myself, I lay back in my corner for some time, nodding to the rhythmical throb of the express as it hurled itself forward through the darkness. Now and again as we shot through some brilliantly illuminated station or past a line of flaming furnaces, I caught for an instant a glimpse of Holmes's figure coiled up snugly in the far corner with his head sunk upon his breast.

It was not until after we had passed Nottingham that I really fell asleep and, when a more than usually violent lurch of the train over some points woke me again, it was broad daylight, and Holmes was sitting up, busy with a Bradshaw and boat timetable. As I moved, he glanced across at me.

"If I'm not mistaken, Watson, that was the Dore and Totley tunnel through which we have just come, and if so we shall be in Sheffield in a few minutes. As you see, I've not been wasting my time altogether, but studying my Bradshaw, which, by the way, Watson, is the most useful book published, without exception, to anyone of my calling."

"How can it possibly help you now?" I asked in some surprise.

"Well, it may or it may not," said Holmes thoughtfully. "But in any case it's well to have at one's finger tips all knowledge which may be of use. It's quite probable that this Jabez Booth may have decided to leave the country and, if this supposition is correct, he would undoubtedly time his little escapade in conformity with information contained in this useful volume. Now, I learn from this Sheffield *Telegraph,* which I obtained at Leicester, by the way, when you were fast asleep, that Mr. Booth cashed the last of his forged cheques at the North British Bank in Saville Street at precisely two-fifteen P.M. on Wednesday last. He made the round of the various banks he visited in a hansom, and it would take him about three minutes only to get from this bank to the G.C. station. From what I gather of the order in which the different banks were visited, he made a circuit, finishing at the nearest point to the G.C. station, at which he could arrive at about two-eighteen. Now, I find that at two-twenty-two a boat express would leave Sheffield G.C., due in Liverpool at four-twenty, and in connection with it the White Star liner *Empress Queen* should have sailed from Liverpool docks at six-thirty for New York. Or again at two-forty-five a boat train would leave Sheffield for Hull, at which town it was due at four-thirty, in time to make a connection with the Holland steam packet, *Comet,* sailing at six-thirty for Amsterdam.

"Here we are provided with two not unlikely means of escape, the former being the most probable; but both worth bearing in mind."

Holmes had scarcely finished speaking when the train drew up.

"Nearly five past four," I remarked.

"Yes," said Holmes, "we are exactly one and a half minutes behind time. And now I propose a good breakfast and a cup of strong coffee, for we have at least a couple of hours to spare."

AFTER BREAKFAST we visited first the police station where we learned that no further developments had taken place in the matter we had come to investigate. Mr. Lestrade of Scotland Yard had arrived the previous evening and had taken the case in hand officially.

We obtained the address of Mr. Jervis, the manager of the bank at which Booth had been an employee, and also that of his landlady at Broomhill.

A hansom landed us at Mr. Jervis's house at Fulwood at seven-thirty. Holmes insisted upon my accompanying him, and we were both shown into a spacious drawing room and asked to wait until the banker could see us.

Mr. Jervis, a stout, florid gentleman of about fifty, came puffing into the room in a very short time. An atmosphere of prosperity seemed to envelop, if not actually to emanate from him.

"Pardon me for keeping you waiting, gentlemen," he said, "but the hour is an early one."

"Indeed, Mr. Jervis," said Holmes, "no apology is needed unless it be on our part. It is, however, necessary that I should ask you a few questions concerning this affair of Mr. Booth, before I can proceed in the matter, and that must be our excuse for paying you such an untimely visit."

"I shall be most happy to answer your questions as far as it lies in my power to do so," said the banker, his fat fingers playing with a bunch of seals at the end of his massive gold watch chain.

"When did Mr. Booth first enter your bank?" said Holmes.

"In January 1881."

"Do you know where he lived when he first came to Sheffield?"

"He took lodgings at Ashgate Road, and has, I believe, lived there ever since."

Do you know anything of his history or life before he came to you?"

"Very little, I fear; beyond that his parents were both dead, and that he came to us with the best testimonials from one of the Leeds branches of our bank, I know nothing."

"Did you find him quick and reliable?"

"He was one of the best and smartest men I have ever had in my employ."

"Do you know whether he was conversant with any other language besides English?"

"I feel pretty sure he wasn't. We have one clerk who attends to any foreign correspondence we may have, and I know that Booth has repeatedly passed letters and papers on to him."

"With your experience of banking matters, Mr. Jervis, how long a time do you think he might reasonably have calculated would elapse between the presentation of the forged cheques and their detection?"

"Well, that would depend very largely upon circumstances," said Mr. Jervis. "In the case of a single cheque it might be a week or two, unless the amounts were so large as to call for special inquiry, in which case it would probably never be cashed at all until such inquiry had been made. In the present case, when there were a dozen forged cheques, it was most unlikely that some one of them should not be detected within twenty-four hours and so lead to the discovery of the fraud. No sane person would dare to presume upon the crime remaining undetected for a longer period than that."

"Thanks," said Holmes, rising. "Those were the chief

points I wished to speak to you about. I will communicate to
you any news of importance I may have."

"I am deeply obliged to you, Mr. Holmes. The case is
naturally causing us great anxiety. We leave it entirely to
your discretion to take whatever steps you may consider
best. Oh, by the way, I sent instructions to Booth's landlady
to disturb nothing in his rooms until you had had an
opportunity of examining them."

"That was a very wise thing to do," said Holmes, "and
may be the means of helping us materially."

"I am also instructed by my company," said the banker,
as he bowed us politely out, "to ask you to make a note of
any expenses incurred, which they will of course immediately
defray."

A FEW MOMENTS LATER we were ringing the bell of the house
in Ashgate Road, Broomhill, at which Mr. Booth had been a
lodger for over seven years. It was answered by a maid who
informed us that Mrs. Purnell was engaged with a gentleman upstairs. When we explained our errand she showed us
at once up to Mr. Booth's rooms, on the first floor, where we
found Mrs. Purnell, a plump, voluble, little lady of about
forty, in conversation with Mr. Lestrade, who appeared to
be just concluding his examination of the rooms.

"Good morning, Holmes," said the detective, with a
very self-satisfied air. "You arrive on the scene a little too
late; I fancy I have already got all the information needed to
catch our man!"

"I'm delighted to hear it," said Holmes dryly, "and must
indeed congratulate you, if this is actually the case. Perhaps
after I've made a little tour of inspection we can compare
notes."

"Just as you please," said Lestrade, with the air of one
who can afford to be gracious. "Candidly, I think you will be

wasting time, and so would you if you knew what I've discovered."

"Still, I must ask you to humour my little whim," said Holmes, leaning against the mantelpiece and whistling softly as he looked round the room.

After a moment he turned to Mrs. Purnell. "The furniture of this room belongs, of course, to you?"

Mrs. Purnell assented.

"The picture that was taken down from over the mantelpiece last Wednesday morning," continued Holmes, "that belonged to Mr. Booth, I presume?"

I followed Holmes's glance across to where an unfaded patch on the wallpaper clearly indicated that a picture had recently been hanging. Well as I knew my friend's methods of reasoning, however, I did not realize for a moment that the little bits of spiderweb which had been behind the picture, and were still clinging to the wall, had told him that the picture could only have been taken down immediately before Mrs. Purnell had received orders to disturb nothing in the room; otherwise her brush, evidently busy enough elsewhere, would not have spared them.

The good lady stared at Sherlock Holmes in open-mouthed astonishment. "Mr. Booth took it down himself on Wednesday morning," she said. "It was a picture he had painted himself, and he thought no end of it. He wrapped it up and took it out with him, remarking that he was going to give it to a friend. I was very much surprised at the time, for I knew he valued it very much; in fact he once told me that he wouldn't part with it for anything. Of course, it's easy to see now why he got rid of it."

"Yes," said Holmes. "It wasn't a large picture, I see. Was it a water colour?"

"Yes, a painting of a stretch of moorland, with three or four large rocks arranged like a big table on a bare hilltop. Druidicals, Mr. Booth called them, or something like that."

"Did Mr. Booth do much painting, then?" enquired Holmes.

"None, whilst he's been here, sir. He has told me he used to do a good deal as a lad, but he had given it up."

Holmes's eyes were glancing round the room again, and an exclamation of surprise escaped him as they encountered a photo standing on the piano.

"Surely that's a photograph of Mr. Booth," he said. "It exactly resembles the description I have of him?"

"Yes," said Mrs. Purnell, "and a very good one it is too."

"How long has it been taken?" said Holmes, picking it up.

"Oh, only a few weeks, sir. I was here when the boy from the photographer's brought them up. Mr. Booth opened the packet whilst I was in the room. There were only two photos, that one and another which he gave to me."

"You interest me exceedingly," said Holmes. "This striped lounge suit he is wearing. Is it the same that he had on when he left Wednesday morning?"

"Yes, he was dressed just like that, as far as I can remember."

"Do you recollect anything of importance that Mr. Booth said to you last Wednesday before he went out?"

"Not very much, I'm afraid, sir. When I took his cup of chocolate up to his bedroom, he said——"

"One moment," interrupted Holmes. "Did Mr. Booth usually have a cup of chocolate in the morning?"

"Oh, yes, sir, summer and winter alike. He was very particular about it and would ring for it as soon as ever he waked. I believe he'd rather have gone without his breakfast almost than have missed his cup of chocolate. Well, as I was saying, sir, I took it up to him myself on Wednesday morning, and he made some remark about the weather and then, just as I was leaving the room, he said, 'Oh, by the way, Mrs. Purnell, I shall be going away tonight for a couple of weeks. I've packed my bag and will call for it this afternoon.' "

"No doubt you were very much surprised at this sudden announcement?" queried Holmes.

"Not very much, sir. Ever since he's had this auditing work to do for the branch banks, there's been no knowing when he would be away. Of course, he'd never been off for two weeks at a stretch, except at holiday times, but he had so often been away for a few days at a time that I had got used to his popping off with hardly a moment's notice."

"Let me see, how long has he had this extra work at the bank — several months, hasn't he?"

"More. It was about last Christmas, I believe, when they gave it to him."

"Oh, yes, of course," said Holmes carelessly, "and this work naturally took him from home a good deal?"

"Yes, indeed, and it seemed to quite tire him, so much evening and night work too, you see, sir. It was enough to knock him out, for he was always such a very quiet, retiring gentleman and hardly ever used to go out in the evenings before."

"Has Mr. Booth left many of his possessions behind him?" asked Holmes.

"Very few, indeed, and what he has are mostly old useless things. But he's a most honest thief, sir," said Mrs. Purnell paradoxically, "and paid me his rent, before he went out on Wednesday morning, right up to next Saturday, because he wouldn't be back by then."

"That was good of him," said Holmes, smiling thoughtfully. "By the way, do you happen to know if he gave away any other treasures before he left?"

"Well, not *just* before, but during the last few months he's taken away most of his books and sold them, I think, a few at a time. He had rather a fancy for old books and has told me that some editions he had were worth quite a lot."

During this conversation, Lestrade had been sitting drumming his fingers impatiently on the table. Now he got up. "Really, I fear I shall have to leave you to this gossip," he said. "I must go and wire instructions for the arrest of Mr. Booth. If only you would have looked before at this old blotter, which I found in the wastebasket, you would have saved yourself a good deal of unnecessary trouble, Mr. Holmes," and he triumphantly slapped down a sheet of well-used blotting paper on the table.

Holmes picked it up and held it in front of a mirror over the sideboard. Looking over his shoulder I could plainly read the reflected impression of a note written in Mr. Booth's handwriting, of which Holmes had procured samples.

It was to a booking agency in Liverpool, giving instructions to them to book a first-class private cabin and passage on board the *Empress Queen* from Liverpool to New York. Parts of the note were slightly obliterated by other impressions, but it went on to say that a cheque was enclosed to pay for tickets, etc., and it was signed by J. Booth.

Holmes stood silently scrutinizing the paper for several minutes.

It was a well-used sheet, but fortunately the impression of the note was well in the centre, and hardly obliterated at all by the other marks and blots, which were all round the outer circumference of the paper. In one corner the address of the Liverpool booking agency was plainly decipherable, the paper evidently having been used to blot the envelope with also.

"My dear Lestrade, you have indeed been more fortunate than I had imagined," said Holmes at length, handing the paper back to him. "May I ask what steps you propose to take next?"

"I shall cable at once to the New York police to arrest the fellow as soon as he arrives," said Lestrade, "but first I must make quite certain the boat doesn't touch at Queenstown or anywhere and give him a chance of slipping through our fingers."

"It doesn't," said Holmes quietly. "I had already looked to see as I thought it not unlikely, at first, that Mr. Booth might have intended to sail by the *Empress Queen.*"

Lestrade gave me a wink for which I would dearly have liked to have knocked him down, for I could see that he disbelieved my friend. I felt a keen pang of disappointment that Holmes's foresight should have been eclipsed in this way by what, after all, was mere good luck on Lestrade's part.

Holmes had turned to Mrs. Purnell and was thanking her.

"Don't mention it, sir," she said. "Mr. Booth deserves to be caught, though I must say he's always been a gentleman to me. I only wish I could have given you some more useful information."

"On the contrary," said Holmes, "I can assure you that what you have told us has been of the utmost importance and will very materially help us. It's just occurred to me, by the way, to wonder if you could possibly put up my friend Dr. Watson and myself for a few days, until we have had time to look into this little matter?"

"Certainly, sir, I shall be most happy."

"Good," said Holmes. "Then you may expect us back to dinner about seven."

WHEN we got outside, Lestrade at once announced his intention of going to the police office and arranging for the necessary orders for Booth's detention and arrest to be cabled to the head of the New York police; Holmes retained an enigmatical silence as to what he proposed to do but expressed his determination to remain at Broomhill and make a few further inquiries. He insisted, however, upon going alone.

"Remember, Watson, you are here for a rest and holiday and I can assure you that if you did remain with me you would only find my program a dull one. Therefore, I insist upon your finding some more entertaining way of spending the remainder of the day."

Past experience told me that it was quite useless to remonstrate or argue with Holmes when once his mind was made up, so I consented with the best grace I could, and leaving Holmes, drove off in the hansom, which he assured me he would not require further.

I passed a few hours in the art gallery and museum and then, after lunch, had a brisk walk out on the Manchester Road and enjoyed the fresh air and moorland scenery, returning to Ashgate Road at seven with better appetite than I had been blessed with for months.

Holmes had not returned, and it was nearly half past seven before he came in. I could see at once that he was in one of his most reticent moods, and all my inquiries failed to elicit any particulars of how he had passed his time or what he thought about the case.

The whole evening he remained coiled up in an easy chair, puffing at his pipe, and hardly a word could I get from him.

His inscrutable countenance and persistent silence gave me no clue whatever as to his thought on the enquiry he had in hand, although I could see his whole mind was concentrated upon it.

NEXT MORNING, just as we had finished breakfast, the maid entered with a note. "From Mr. Jervis, sir; there's no answer," she said.

Holmes tore open the envelope and scanned the note hurriedly and, as he did so, I noticed a flush of annoyance spread over his usually pale face.

"Confound his impudence," he muttered. "Read that,

Watson. I don't ever remember to have been treated so badly in a case before."

The note was a brief one:

The Cedars, Fulwood.
September sixth

Mr. Jervis, on behalf of the directors of the British Consolidated Bank, begs to thank Mr. Sherlock Holmes for his prompt attention and valued services in the matter concerning the fraud and disappearance of their ex-employee, Mr. Jabez Booth.

Mr. Lestrade, of Scotland Yard, informs us that he has succeeded in tracking the individual in question who will be arrested shortly. Under these circumstances they feel it unnecessary to take up any more of Mr. Holmes's valuable time.

"Rather cool, eh, Watson? I'm much mistaken if they don't have cause to regret their action when it's too late. After this I shall certainly refuse to act for them any further in the case, even if they ask me to do so. In a way I'm sorry because the matter presented some distinctly interesting features and is by no means the simple affair our friend Lestrade thinks."

"Why, don't you think he is on the right scent?" I exclaimed.

"Wait and see, Watson," said Holmes mysteriously. "Mr. Booth hasn't been caught yet, remember." And that was all that I could get out of him.

One result of the summary way in which the banker had dispensed with my friend's services was that Holmes and I spent a most restful and enjoyable week in the small village of Hathersage, on the edge of the Derbyshire moors, and returned to London feeling better for our long moorland rambles.

Holmes having very little work in hand at the time, and

my wife not yet having returned from her Swiss holiday, I prevailed upon him, though not without considerable difficulty, to pass the next few weeks with me instead of returning to his rooms at Baker Street.

Of course, we watched the development of the Sheffield forgery case with the keenest interest. Somehow the particulars of Lestrade's discoveries got into the papers, and the day after we left Sheffield they were full of the exciting chase of Mr. Booth, the man wanted for the Sheffield bank frauds.

They spoke of "the guilty man restlessly pacing the deck of the *Empress Queen,* as she ploughed her way majestically across the solitary wastes of the Atlantic, all unconscious that the inexorable hand of justice could stretch over the ocean and was already waiting to seize him on his arrival in the New World." And Holmes after reading these sensational paragraphs would always lay down the paper with one of his enigmatical smiles.

At last the day on which the *Empress Queen* was due at New York arrived, and I could not help but notice that even Holmes's usually inscrutable face wore a look of suppressed excitement as he unfolded the evening paper. But our surprise was doomed to be prolonged still further. There was a brief paragraph to say that the *Empress Queen* had arrived off Long Island at six A.M. after a good passage. There was, however, a case of cholera on board, and the New York authorities had consequently been compelled to put the boat in quarantine, and none of the passengers or crew would be allowed to leave her for a period of twelve days.

Two days later there was a full column in the papers stating that it had been definitely ascertained that Mr. Booth was really on board the *Empress Queen.* He had been identified and spoken to by one of the sanitary inspectors who had had to visit the boat. He was being kept under close observation, and there was no possible chance of his escaping. Mr. Lestrade of Scotland Yard, by whom Booth had been so cleverly tracked down and his escape forestalled, had taken passage on the *Oceania,* due in New York on the tenth, and would personally arrest Mr. Booth when he was allowed to land.

Never before or since have I seen my friend Holmes so astonished as when he had finished reading this announcement. I could see that he was thoroughly mystified, though why he should be so was quite a puzzle to me. All day he sat coiled up in an easy chair, with his brows drawn down into two hard lines and his eyes half closed as he puffed away at his oldest brier in silence.

"Watson," he said once, glancing across at me, "it's perhaps a good thing that I was asked to drop that Sheffield case. As things are turning out I fancy I should only have made a fool of myself."

"Why?" I asked.

"Because I began by assuming that somebody else wasn't one—and now it looks as though I had been mistaken."

For the next few days Holmes seemed quite depressed, for nothing annoyed him more than to feel that he had made any mistake in his deductions or got onto a false line of reasoning.

At last the fatal tenth of September, the day on which Booth was to be arrested, arrived. Eagerly but in vain we scanned the evening papers. The morning of the eleventh came and still brought no news of the arrest, but in the evening papers of that day there was a short paragraph hinting that the criminal had escaped again.

For several days the papers were full of the most conflicting rumours and conjectures as to what had actually taken place, but all were agreed in affirming that Mr. Lestrade was on his way home alone and would be back in Liverpool on the seventeenth or eighteenth.

On the evening of the last named day Holmes and I sat smoking in his Baker Street rooms, when his boy came in to announce that Mr. Lestrade of Scotland Yard was below and would like the favour of a few minutes' conversation.

"Show him up, show him up," said Holmes, rubbing his hands together with an excitement quite unusual to him.

Lestrade entered the room and sat down in the seat to which Holmes waved him, with a most dejected air.

"It's not often I'm at fault, Mr. Holmes," he began, "but in this Sheffield business I've been beaten hollow."

"Dear me," said Holmes pleasantly, "you surely don't mean to tell me that you haven't got your man yet."

"I do," said Lestrade. "What's more, I don't think he ever will be caught!"

"Don't despair so soon," said Holmes encouragingly. "After you have told us all that's already happened, it's just within the bounds of possibility that I may be able to help you with some little suggestions."

Thus encouraged, Lestrade began his strange story to which we both listened with breathless interest.

"It's quite unnecessary for me to dwell upon incidents which are already familiar," he said. "You know of the discovery I made in Sheffield which, of course, convinced me that the man I wanted had sailed for New York on the *Empress Queen*. I was in a fever of impatience for his arrest, and when I heard that the boat he had taken passage on had been placed in quarantine, I set off at once in order that I might actually lay hands upon him myself. Never have five days seemed so long.

"We reached New York on the evening of the ninth, and I rushed off at once to the head of the New York police and from him learned that there was no doubt whatever that Mr. Jabez Booth was indeed on board the *Empress Queen*. One of the sanitary inspectors who had had to visit the boat had not only seen but actually spoken to him. The man exactly answered the description of Booth which had appeared in the papers. One of the New York detectives had been sent on board to make a few inquiries and to inform the captain privately of the impending arrest. He found that Mr. Jabez Booth had actually had the audacity to book his passage and travel under his real name without even attempting to disguise himself in any way. He had a private first-class cabin, and the purser declared that he had been suspicious of the man from the first. He had kept himself shut up in his cabin nearly all the time, posing as an eccentric semi-invalid person who must not be disturbed on any account. Most of his meals had been sent down to his cabin, and he had been seen on deck but seldom and hardly ever dined with the rest of the passengers. It was quite evident that he had been trying to keep out of sight, and to attract as little attention as possible. The stewards and some of the passengers who were approached on the subject later were all agreed that this was the case.

"It was decided that during the time the boat was in quarantine nothing should be said to Booth to arouse his suspicions but that the pursers, steward, and captain, who were the only persons in the secret, should between them keep him under observation until the tenth, the day on which passengers would be allowed to leave the boat. On that day he should be arrested."

Here we were interrupted by Holmes's boy, who came in with a telegram. Holmes glanced at it with a faint smile.

"No answer," he said, slipping it in his waistcoat pocket. "Pray continue your very interesting story, Lestrade."

"Well, on the afternoon of the tenth, accompanied by the New York chief inspector of police and detective Forsyth," resumed Lestrade, "I went on board the *Empress Queen* half an hour before she was due to come up to the landing stage to allow passengers to disembark.

"The purser informed us that Mr. Booth had been on deck and that he had been in conversation with him about fifteen minutes before our arrival. He had then gone down to his cabin and the purser, making some excuse to go down also, had actually seen him enter it. He had been standing

near the top of the companionway since then and was sure
Booth had not come up on deck again since.

"'At last,' I muttered to myself, as we all went down
below, led by the purser, who took us straight to Booth's
cabin. We knocked but, getting no answer, tried the door
and found it locked. The purser assured us, however, that
this was nothing unusual. Mr. Booth had had his cabin door
locked a good deal and, often, even his meals had been left
on a tray outside. We held a hurried consultation and, as
time was short, decided to force the door. Two good blows
with a heavy hammer broke it from the hinges, and we all
rushed in. You can picture our astonishment when we found
the cabin empty. We searched it thoroughly, and Booth was
certainly not there."

"One moment," interrupted Holmes. "The key of the
door — was it on the inside of the lock or not?"

"It was nowhere to be seen," said Lestrade. "I was
getting frantic for, by this time, I could feel the vibration of
the engines and hear the first churning sound of the screw as
the great boat began to slide slowly down towards the
landing stage.

"We were at our wits' end; Mr. Booth must be hiding
somewhere on board, but there was now no time to make a
proper search for him, and in a very few minutes passengers
would be leaving the boat. At last the captain promised us
that, under the circumstances, only one landing gangway
should be run out and, in company with the purser and
stewards, I should stand by it with a complete list of
passengers, ticking off each one as he or she left. By this
means it would be quite impossible for Booth to escape us
even if he attempted some disguise, for no person whatever
would be allowed to cross the gangway until identified by the
purser or one of the stewards.

"I was delighted with the arrangement, for there was
now no way by which Booth could give me the slip.

"One by one the passengers crossed the gangway and

joined the jostling crowd on the landing stage and each one was identified and his or her name crossed off my list. There were one hundred and ninety-three first-class passengers on board the *Empress Queen,* including Booth, and, when one hundred and ninety-two had disembarked, his was the only name which remained!

"You can scarcely realize what a fever of impatience we were in," said Lestrade, mopping his brow at the very recollection, "nor how interminable the time seemed as we slowly but carefully ticked off one by one the whole of the three hundred and twenty-four second-class passengers and the three hundred and ten steerage from my list. Every passenger except Mr. Booth crossed that gangway, but he certainly did not do so. There was no possible room for doubt on that point.

"He must therefore be still on the boat, we agreed, but I was getting panic-stricken and wondered if there were any possibility of his getting smuggled off in some of the luggage which the great cranes were now beginning to swing up onto the pier.

"I hinted my fear to detective Forsyth, and he at once arranged that every trunk or box in which there was any chance for a man to hide should be opened and examined by the customs officers.

"It was a tedious business, but they didn't shirk it, and at the end of two hours were able to assure us that by no possibility could Booth have been smuggled off the boat in this way.

"This left only one possible solution to the mystery. He *must* be still in hiding somewhere on board. We had had the boat kept under the closest observation ever since she came up to the landing stage, and now the superintendent of police lent us a staff of twenty men and, with the consent of the captain and the assistance of the pursers and stewards, etc., the *Empress Queen* was searched and re-searched from stem to stern. We didn't leave unexamined a place in which a cat could have hidden, but the missing man wasn't there. Of that I'm certain — and there you have the whole mystery in a nutshell, Mr. Holmes. Mr. Booth certainly *was* on board the *Empress Queen* up to, and at, eleven o'clock on the morning of the tenth, and although he could not by any possibility have left it, we are nevertheless face to face with the fact that he wasn't there at five o'clock in the afternoon."

LESTRADE'S FACE, as he concluded his curious and mysterious narrative, bore a look of the most hopeless bewilderment I ever saw, and I fancy my own must have pretty well matched it, but Holmes threw himself back in his easy chair, with his long thin legs stuck straight out in front of him, his whole frame literally shaking with silent laughter. "What conclusion have you come to?" he gasped at length. "What steps do you propose to take next?"

"I've no idea. Who could know what to do? The whole thing is impossible, perfectly impossible; it's an insoluble mystery. I came to you to see if you could, by any chance, suggest some entirely fresh line of inquiry upon which I might begin to work."

"Well," said Holmes, cocking his eye mischievously at the bewildered Lestrade, "I can give you Booth's present address, if it will be of any use to you?"

"His what!" cried Lestrade.

"His present address," repeated Holmes quietly. "But before I do so, my dear Lestrade, I must make one stipulation. Mr. Jervis has treated me very shabbily in the matter, and I don't desire that my name shall be associated with it any further. Whatever you do you must not hint the source from which any information I may give you has come. You promise?"

"Yes," murmured Lestrade, who was in a state of bewildered excitement.

Holmes tore a leaf from his pocket book and scribbled

on it: Mr. A. Winter, c/o Mrs. Thackary, Glossop Road, Broomhill, Sheffield.

"You will find there the present name and address of the man you are in search of," he said, handing the paper across to Lestrade. "I should strongly advise you to lose no time in getting hold of him, for though the wire I received a short time ago — which unfortunately interrupted your most interesting narrative — was to tell me that Mr. Winter had arrived back home again after a temporary absence, still it's more than probable that he will leave there, for good, at an early date. I can't say how soon — not for a few days, I should think."

Lestrade rose. "Mr. Holmes, you're a brick," he said, with more real feeling than I have ever seen him show before. "You've saved my reputation in this job just when I was beginning to look like a perfect fool, and now you're forcing me to take all the credit, when I don't deserve one atom. As to how you have found this out, it's as great a mystery to me as Booth's disappearance was."

"Well, as to that," said Holmes airily, "I can't be sure of all the facts myself, for of course I've never looked properly into the case. But they are pretty easy to conjecture, and I shall be most happy to give you my idea of Booth's trip to New York on some future occasion when you have more time to spare.

"By the way," called out Holmes, as Lestrade was leaving the room, "I shouldn't be surprised if you find Mr. Jabez Booth, *alias* Mr. Archibald Winter, a slight acquaintance of yours, for he would undoubtedly be a fellow passenger of yours, on your homeward journey from America. He reached Sheffield a few hours before you arrived in London and, as he has certainly just returned from New York, like yourself, it's evident you must have crossed on the same boat. He would be wearing smoked glasses and have a heavy dark moustache."

"Ah!" said Lestrade, "there *was* a man called Winter on

board who answered to that description. I believe it must have been he, and I'll lose no more time," and Lestrade hurried off.

"WELL, Watson, my boy, you look nearly as bewildered as our friend Lestrade," said Holmes, leaning back in his chair and looking roguishly across at me, as he lighted his old brier pipe.

"I must confess that none of the problems you have had to solve, in the past, seemed more inexplicable to me than Lestrade's account of Booth's disappearance from the *Empress Queen*."

"Yes, that part of the story is decidedly neat," chuckled Holmes, "but I'll tell you how I got at the solution of the mystery. I see you are ready to listen.

"The first thing to do in any case is to gauge the intelligence and cunning of the criminal. Now, Mr. Booth was undoubtedly a clever man. Mr. Jervis himself, you remember, assured us as much. The fact that he opened banking accounts in preparation for the crime twelve months before he committed it proves it to have been a long-premeditated one. I began the case, therefore, with the knowledge that I had a clever man to catch, who had had twelve months in which to plan his escape.

"My first real clues came from Mrs. Purnell," said Holmes. "Most important were her remarks about Booth's auditing work which kept him from home so many days and nights, often consecutively. I felt certain at once, and inquiry confirmed, that Mr. Booth had had no such extra work at all. Why then had he invented lies to explain these absences to his landlady? Probably because they were in some way connected, either with the crime, or with his plans for escaping after he had committed it. It was inconceivable that so much mysterious outdoor occupation could be directly connected with the forgery, and I at once deduced that this time had been spent by Booth in paving the way for his escape.

"Almost at once the idea that he had been living a double life occurred to me, his intention doubtless being to quietly drop one individuality after committing the crime and permanently take up the other—a far safer and less clumsy expedient than the usual one of assuming a new disguise just at the moment when everybody is expecting and looking for you to do so.

"Then there were the interesting facts relating to Booth's picture and books. I tried to put myself in his place. He valued these possessions highly; they were light and portable, and there was really no reason whatever why he should part with them. Doubtless, then, he had taken them away by degrees and put them someplace where he could lay hands on them again. If I could find out where this place was, I felt sure there would be every chance I could catch him when he attempted to recover them.

"The picture couldn't have gone far for he had taken it out with him on the very day of the crime . . . I needn't bore you with details . . . I was two hours making inquiries before I found the house at which he had called and left it—which was none other than Mrs. Thackary's in Glossop Road.

"I made a pretext for calling there and found Mrs. T. one of the most easy mortals in the world to pump. In less than half an hour I knew that she had a boarder named Winter, that he professed to be a commercial traveler and was from home most of the time. His description resembled Booth's save that he had a mustache, wore glasses.

"As I've often tried to impress upon you before, Watson, details are the most important things of all, and it gave me a real thrill of pleasure to learn that Mr. Winter had a cup of chocolate brought up to his bedroom every morning. A gentleman called on the Wednesday morning and left a parcel, saying it was a picture he had promised for Mr. Winter, and asking Mrs. Thackary to give it to Winter when he returned. Mr. Winter had taken the rooms the previous December. He had a good many books which he had brought in from time to time. All these facts taken in conjunction made me certain that I was on the right scent. Winter and Booth were one and the same person, and as soon as Booth had put all his pursuers off the track he would return, as Winter, and repossess his treasures.

"The newly taken photo and the old blotter with its telltale note were too obviously intentional means of drawing the police onto Booth's track. The blotter, I could see almost at once, was a fraud, for not only would it be almost impossible to use one in the ordinary way so much without the central part becoming undecipherable, but I could see where it had been touched up.

"I concluded therefore that Booth, *alias* Winter, never actually intended to sail on the *Empress Queen,* but in that I underestimated his ingenuity. Evidently he booked *two* berths on the boat, one in his real, and one in his assumed name, and managed very cleverly to successfully keep up the two characters throughout the voyage, appearing first as one individual and then as the other. Most of the time he posed as Winter, and for this purpose Booth became the eccentric semi-invalid passenger who remained locked up in his cabin for such a large part of his time. This, of course, would answer his purpose well; his eccentricity would only draw attention to his presence on board and so make him one of the best-known passengers on the boat, although he showed so little of himself.

"I had left instructions with Mrs. Thackary to send me a wire as soon as Winter returned. When Booth had led his pursuers to New York, and there thrown them off the scent, he had nothing more to do but to take the first boat back. Very naturally it chanced to be the same as that on which our friend Lestrade returned, and that was how Mrs. Thackary's wire arrived at the opportune moment it did."

Arthur Whitaker (1882–1949): retired architect, amateur ornithologist, and the true author of "The Man Who Was Wanted"—a story which might be included in the Sherlock Holmes Canon today, had he not persisted despite adversity in setting the record straight. (Courtesy of Richard Lancelyn Green)

Adrian M. Conan Doyle (1910–1970), *circa* 1940. Although his brother Denis was senior to Adrian in managing the Conan Doyle Estate, the strong-willed, impulsive, and litigious Adrian set the pace in the case of "The Man Who Was Wanted" and most other Conan Doyle controversies. (Courtesy of Richard Lancelyn Green)

Denis P. S. Conan Doyle (1909–1955), also *circa* 1940. Upon his mother's death that year, he became the head of the Conan Doyle Estate and spent much of the 1940s in the United States and elsewhere attending to the Estate's business affairs. (Courtesy of Richard Lancelyn Green)

Woods Place,
Battle,
Sussex.

27 Feb. 1944.

Dear G.B.S.,

I wonder if you'd mind glancing through the enclosed and giving me your advice?

The first enclosure is a copy of a letter I received from Conan Doyle's son Adrian when I sent him my Life of his father.

The second is a copy of a letter I have only just received from him.

The third is my suggested reply, which I won't send for a week or so in case you can suggest a better.

Adrian is obviously insane: he sees no fault in his father, and k on at least two occasions he wrote abusive letters to critics of my book who had implied that his father was a bit of an ass. He also wrote to the press saying that I was wrong in my assumption that Dr Watson resembled his father, who, he declared, was Sherlock Holmes to the life! *What a libel! Sherlock was a drug addict without a single amiable trait, and Watson a decent fellow*

This is his latest bombshell, possibly due to spiritualistic pressure acting on his natural pateritis.

He let me run through his father's papers, for which reason I don't wish to send up his bloodpresssure; but his latest letter is a bit thick. *(An excellent advertisement for another edition - /*

What more can he do than send another manifesto to the papers dissociating his family, and possibly the deity, from my book?

But how on earth does one treat a madman like this? A soft answer is supposed to turn away wrath, but I fancy a bludgeon is best for a bedlamite. *Suggestion enclosed.*

Yours ever

Hesketh

Hesketh Pearson (1887–1964): "a wicked man whose opinions on the sacred subject were too monstrous to be considered," as he correctly described Denis and Adrian Conan Doyle's view in a January 2, 1949, letter to Vincent Starrett.

Vincent Starrett as Sherlock Holmes, drawn by *Chicago Tribune* staff artist Ben Cohen for the newspaper's in-house account of how the story of "The Man Who Was Wanted" was broken. (Courtesy of the late Michael Murphy)

The copy of the August 1948 *Cosmopolitan* which Vincent Starrett sent to Hesketh Pearson (note the inscription in the upper right-hand corner). The Baker Street Irregulars challenged the story's authenticity—and Pearson knew who had really written it. (Courtesy of Richard Lancelyn Green)

THE MAN WHO WAS WANTED.

During the late autumn of 95 a fortunate chance enabled me to take some part in another of my friend Sherlock Holmes' fascinating cases. My wife not having been well for some time , I had at last persuaded her to take a holiday if Switzerland in the company of her old school friend Kate Whitney,—whose name may be remembered in connection with the strange case I have already chronicled under the title of "The Man with the Twisted Lip". My practice had grown much and I had been working very hard for many months and never felt in more need myself of a rest and a holiday. Unfortunately I dare not absent myself for a long enough period to warrant a visit to the Alps. I promised my wife, however, that I would get a week or ten days holiday in somehow, and it was only on this understanding that she consented to the Swiss tour I was so anxious for her to take. One of my best patients was in a very critical state at the time and it was not until August was gone that he passed the crisis and began to recover. Feeling then that I could leave my practice with a good conscience in the hands of a locum tenens , I began to wonder where and how I should best find the rest and change I needed.

Almost at once the idea came to my mind that I would hunt up my old friend Sherlock Holmes, whom I had seen nothing of for several months, if he had no important enquiery in hand I would do my uttermost to persuade him to join me.

Within half an hour of coming to this resolution I was standing in the doorway of the familiar old room in Baker St.

Holmes was stretched upon ~~her/his~~ the couch with his back towards me, the familiar dressing gown and old briar pipe as much in evidence as of yore.

Arthur Whitaker's carbon copy of "The Man Who Was Wanted,"
which he had kept all those years, matched the "Conan Doyle"
typescript in Adrian's possession. (Courtesy of Richard Lancelyn
Green)

[51]

WINDLESHAM,

CROWBOROUGH,

SUSSEX.

March 7/11

Dear Sir

I read your story. It is not bad & I don't see why you should not change the names, and try to get it published yourself. Of course you could not use the names of my characters.

It is impossible for me to join with another in any case for the result would be that any price would at once be knocked down 75 per cent by Editors.

Sometimes I am open to purchase ideas which I lay aside and use at my own time in my own way. I did this once before and gave 10 guineas for the idea, working it out my own lines. If you wished I would do this for you, but I could not guarantee ever to use it,

Arthur Conan Doyle's March 7, 1911, letter to Arthur Whitaker eliminated any lingering doubts that Adrian might have had about the story's authorship. (Courtesy of Richard Lancelyn Green)

Arthur Conan Doyle in 1929, with his teenaged
sons Adrian (left) and Denis. Their close relation-
ship with their father turned worshipful after his
death the following year, making Adrian in particular a prickly person for critics of Conan Doyle's
life and work to deal with. (Courtesy of Dame Jean
Conan Doyle)

Nova 57 Minor

I

IF the reader is to understand the history of "The Man Who Was Wanted" in all of its color and passion, another story must be told first. The typescript of "The Man Who Was Wanted" was discovered in 1942 by the English writer and biographer Hesketh Pearson during the research for his biography of Sir Arthur Conan Doyle, *Conan Doyle: His Life and Art,* published the following year. In that book, Pearson printed the opening of the unpublished story, telling of

> my discovery among his papers of a complete unpublished Holmes story entitled "The Man Who Was Wanted," which is certainly not up to the mark. . . . The problem and its solution show that Doyle was right to shelve the story, though the fact that he did not destroy it suggests either that he hoped to make the rest of it worthy of the opening or that he wished to make use of the opening in a worthier episode.[1]

Had Hesketh Pearson never been connected with the discovery and publicizing of "The Man Who Was Wanted,"* it is unlikely that the Conan Doyle Estate's reaction would

---

*On a number of occasions, Adrian Conan Doyle claimed to have made the actual discovery while assisting Hesketh Pearson's research — always denying, in subsequent years, that Pearson had had any access to his father's archives.

57

have been so extreme when the story's true authorship came
to light several years later. For by then, the Conan Doyle
Estate, and particularly Adrian Conan Doyle among the
deceased author's children, bore a considerable animus
against Hesketh Pearson.

Pearson had not set out to debunk Sir Arthur Conan
Doyle in his biography. On the contrary, his diary entry for
November 18, 1941, recorded considerable affection for the
author and his fiction:

> I think he wants "placing" in the literary firma-
> ment, and so far he has been regarded as an
> elaborate joke by highbrows, who patronize him
> but funk a real assessment . . . [W]hen the object
> of reading is to rest, refresh or recreate the mind,
> no volumes in our literature are so welcome as
> those which constitute the *Holmes* saga, the *Gerard*
> stories, and *Rodney Stone*. We could better spare an
> equivalent output by any better writer of fiction, if
> such there be.[2]

He lunched with Adrian Conan Doyle at the Savage Club in
London early in 1942 and came away convinced that Adrian
was "a charming fellow who offers to do everything for me to
help in my life of his father."[3] But relations turned sour after
the biography came out. The story of the dispute between
the biographer and his subject's touchy son has been told
quite well by Michael Holroyd, Hesketh Pearson's literary
executor and the biographer of George Bernard Shaw, in his
valuable article "Hesketh Pearson: Biography with Warts."[4]
Only a brief summary is needed here, to illustrate Adrian's
attitude toward Hesketh Pearson.

When Pearson's biography of Sir Arthur was brought out
in September 1943, Adrian's tone was congratulatory at
first: "[T]hough I violently disagree with many of your
opinions, the book is *splendid*," he wrote Pearson on

September 24, 1943 (emphasis in the original).[5] As early as the following month, however, a certain cooling process had begun. To Adrian's dismay and anger, a number of reviewers, beginning with G. W. Stonier in *The New Statesman* of September 15, 1943, were focusing upon what they took to be Sir Arthur's Watsonish qualities, and upon Pearson's all-interpretive use of Sir Arthur's satirical self-description as "the man in the street."

At first, Adrian vented his ire upon the reviewers. A short but very stiff letter went out to Stonier on October 6, 1943, and, in a letter to Hesketh Pearson that same day, the volatile Adrian wrote:

> Having read his anything but complimentary references to yourself and Hugh Kingsmill,* followed by the insultingly worded froth against my father and his best works, I can only say with all sincerity, that I deeply regret that in this curiously uncultured country I am forbidden the rights that would be mine in either France or Spain or Italy, to "call this man out," that he might give me every satisfaction for his false and ill-curried references to my great father.[6]

---

*Writer Hugh Kingsmill, author of a well-known early Sherlock Holmes pastiche called "The Ruby of Khitmandu" (*The Bookman* [London], April 1932), was a close friend and literary collaborator of Hesketh Pearson. Together they had authored *Skye High* (Oxford University Press, 1938), a book of conversation which, if Adrian Conan Doyle had read it, might have given him pause before encouraging Pearson to write a biography of his father. In it, Pearson had dismissed Arthur Conan Doyle's serious historical romances as uninteresting, complaining that "none of the persons in [*The White Company*] can stir a step without bumping into material out of Conan Doyle's note-books" (pp. 243–46).

By the end of October, Adrian had prepared a counter-vailing letter for the London newspapers and literary journals under the title of "Sherlock Holmes's Identity — Sir Arthur Conan Doyle Himself." It appeared in *The Times* on October 28, and in several other papers as well. In it, Adrian claimed to have "the highest regard" for Hesketh Pearson, "both as a writer and a friend," but it was obvious that whatever high regard he actually had was wearing thin. Pearson tried to assuage Adrian's concern about his father's reputation in print, in a letter of reply that appeared in *The Times* on November 1, and in other papers, and at first he may have thought he had succeeded, for, on November 9, Adrian wrote to him:

> I am most interested to hear that the book is already sold out and that the new edition will be on the market for Christmas. It is a rightful reward for your long months of reading and work.[7]

But this forebearing attitude did not last. The break came once and for all toward the end of February 1944, when Adrian wrote to Pearson upon returning to Bignell Wood, the Conan Doyles' holiday house in the New Forest, after a recuperative hospital stay following an operation. In his letter of February 20, Adrian claimed to have just read Pearson's biography of his father for the first time, and he was most unhappy with what he had read: "[A]s a portrayal of my father, his background, his character, and his status as a man, it is a travesty." Indeed, Adrian continued,

> the morbid, slow-minded "son of the people" Englishman depicted in your book, a character built on sweeping and entirely unwarranted gen-eralisation and potent omissions, has no relation whatsoever to the character and attributes of the blood-proud man who was my father. If, instead of

blindly accepting the opinions of a few men who had no personal experience of my father whatsoever beyond the merest acquaintanceship, you had taken the ordinary precaution of submitting the manuscript to a member of the family before publication, not for dictatorial ruling but in order that your portrayal might at least be based on fact, then your numerous inaccuracies and, above all, your fundamental omissions would have been avoided.

As it is you will appreciate that, in view of the fact that our father was both a public man and the scion of an ancient House, the family have no intention whatever of allowing the matter to stand in its present disguise.[8]

"Adrian is obviously insane," a flabbergasted Pearson wrote to George Bernard Shaw, another of his biographical subjects, a week later; "he sees no fault in his father, and on at least two occasions he wrote abusive letters to critics of my book who had implied that his father was a bit of an ass."[9]

"Let nothing induce you to argue with this man," was Shaw's advice to Pearson: "It could do no good and be an expensive and very wearing waste of time."[10] Shaw was an old acquaintance of the late Sir Arthur Conan Doyle, and had occasionally crossed swords with him in print. It was he who drafted the reply which Pearson sent to Adrian on March 6,* a guarded letter which expressed regret at his unhappiness, but pointed out that a professional biographer's view of his subject was bound to differ from that of a son; and he welcomed any new light that Adrian might care to shed upon his father in print.

---

* Replacing an earlier draft reply to Adrian that Hugh Kingsmill had written for Pearson.

"But how on earth does one treat a madman like this?"
Pearson had asked Shaw. "A soft answer is supposed to turn
away wrath, but I fancy a bludgeon is best for a bedlamite."[11]
Certainly the soft answer did little good. Not only was
Adrian's anger not quenched, but his older brother Denis
put in his own word (though not until a year later, on March
24, 1945), in a letter from Madrid:

> It is not a biography of my father at all—it is a
> cross between an impertinent caricature and a
> purely imaginary travesty. How you could have
> had the wanton effrontery to publish your book
> without first submitting the MS. to at least one
> member of my father's intimate family passes my
> comprehension, but be that as it may, I do not
> intend to allow the matter to rest as it is.[12]

This "whiff of lawyers," as Michael Holroyd has called it,[13]
came to nothing but threats. The product of Adrian's wrath
turned out to be, not a lawsuit, for there were no grounds for
one, but instead his short booklet called *The True Conan
Doyle,* published by John Murray in 1945. It began with an
attack upon Hesketh Pearson and his biography of Sir
Arthur,* continued with the claim that, though a son, the
author's view of his father was anything but biased, and then

---

*"In its portrayal of my father and his opinions, the book is a
travesty, and the personal values therein ascribed to him are, in
effect, the very antithesis of everything that he represented,
believed in, and held dear. . . . As for the literary aspect, Sir
Arthur's seventy-odd books should manage to survive the drone of
Mr. Pearson's wearisomely condescending criticism."[14] Adrian
sent Pearson a copy of his book which Pearson promptly sold for
nine shillings, "with difficulty resisting the temptation to write and
ask the author for more."[15]

proceeded to deliver some twenty-seven more pages of sheer hagiography.

With this book, he invited the critics to side with his interpretation against Pearson's, both through the fact of its publication and in direct if clandestine approach to such eminent critics as James Agate of *The Sunday Times*. Adrian met with scant success, though. Agate rebuffed his attempt to enlist him as an ally against Pearson. He wrote a long letter to Adrian on October 27, 1945, defending Pearson's capabilities as a biographer, and concluding: "No, Sir, you must make out a stronger case before you enlist my aid in your campaign against H.P.'s sauce."[16] Through his secretary, Agate sent Pearson a terser version of his response: "Mr. Agate thanks you for your letter. He says he has told Conan Doyle to shut up."[17]

And the reviews of *The True Conan Doyle* were cool. Wrote one critic:

> One suspects Mr. Adrian Conan Doyle of a certain lack of humour. The writer of this brochure displays too much asperity. It cannot be doubted that everybody is filled with admiration and gratitude to his father, and with piety and affection for his father's memory, probably none more than Mr. Hesketh Pearson, but that does not mean that competent critics are not entitled to discuss and interpret both the work and the personality of so outstanding a literary figure.[18]

But to Adrian, it seemed to mean just that. And no one had transgressed so grievously, even maliciously, as far as he was concerned, as Hesketh Pearson. The dispute over the biography created a bitter dislike and resentment toward Pearson on Adrian's part that never disappeared.

II

Now to "The Man Who Was Wanted." The first public mention of the story appeared in the anonymous "Star Man's Diary" gossip column of the London *Star* on June 13, 1942. "Admirers of Sherlock Holmes will be interested to learn," it said, in breathtaking understatement, "that the manuscript of an unpublished adventure of the greatest of all fiction detectives has recently been discovered."[19] The source of information was Adrian Conan Doyle, who had been interviewed about the recent deal, concluded with Universal Studios in the United States, for a new series of Sherlock Holmes movies to star Basil Rathbone. A clipping of the *Star* article was sent by London bookseller Bertram Rota to a Baker Street Irregular in Boston named P. M. Stone.[20]

The thrill of learning about a sixty-first adventure of Sherlock Holmes was tremendous — Edgar W. Smith, Commissionaire of the Baker Street Irregulars, said that the discovery was "of cosmic importance"[21] in a letter to the *Saturday Review of Literature* — but there was alarming news in the London *Star* article also. No reason was given for it, but the article reported that the Conan Doyle Estate did not intend to publish the story. Could such a thing possibly, conceivably be true? "In God's name, *why?*" wailed an anguished Vincent Starrett in Chicago.[22] Edgar Smith wrote an agitated letter to the Baker Street Irregulars about it in August, and the news was given wider circulation the following autumn by several Irregulars in the newspaper world — by Vincent Starrett in his very first "Books Alive"

column in the *Chicago Tribune,* calling the new Holmes story
"Nova 57 Minor," and by Anthony Boucher in the *San
Francisco Chronicle.*[23]

The most informative account, however, appeared in the
New York Times of September 13, 1942. This was an Associated Press article that was the work of yet another Baker
Street Irregular, Charles Honce, the AP's news editor, and
the AP's London correspondent, William King. The article
described the discovery of "The Man Who Was Wanted,"
the finding of the manuscript inside an envelope contained
in an old chest full of family papers. (Later accounts in 1947
confused it with other manuscript discoveries, mistakenly
calling the container a hatbox, an error that still crops up
today.) On the envelope had been a note in the handwriting
of Lady Conan Doyle, Sir Arthur's widow (herself deceased
in 1940), to the effect that her husband did not intend to
publish the story because it fell below the standard of his
others. The article quoted both Hesketh Pearson and Adrian
Conan Doyle on the fundamental weakness of the tale. But,
for the first time, Adrian held out some hope that it might be
published one day. "I realize," he said, "that there may be a
great demand from Sherlock Holmes admirers to have the
story published. . . . In that case the family might consent.
I cannot say definitely, however, until my elder brother,
Denis Conan Doyle, returns from America."[24]

The peripatetic Denis was indeed in the United States,
seeing to the Estate's financial interests here. On September
11, 1942, Adrian had written to Hesketh Pearson:

> By the way, I hear from Denis that America is
> shaken by the news of the discovered Holmes
> story. He has been bombarded by letters from the
> various societies all over America, has had to
> broadcast and, of all things on earth, received
> deputations from celebrated American literary

men requesting that the story be published regard-
less of its standard![25]

During the autumn of 1942, Edgar Smith was for a time
sufficiently hopeful about the release of "The Man Who Was
Wanted" by the Conan Doyle Estate that the story played a
part in his negotiations with publishers for his forthcoming
Sherlockian anthology *Profile by Gaslight.* If "The Man Who
Was Wanted" were made available, he told Vincent Starrett
in a letter dated October 16, 1942, Doubleday would publish
the book; if it were not, then Simon & Schuster would be
willing to publish the anthology without it. In the end, the
Conan Doyle Estate continued to withhold the story, and
Profile by Gaslight was published in 1944 by Simon & Schuster.

Denis Conan Doyle had attended the 1940 Baker Street
Irregulars' annual dinner in New York City. He had spoken
there on the subject of "My Father's Friend, Mr. Sherlock
Holmes," and Christopher Morley, the BSI's founder and
Gasogene, later called it "probably the most charming
discourse to which we have listened."[26] * But now he rather
prudently absented himself, in Washington, D.C., from the
1943 BSI annual dinner in New York, which an impatiently
chafing Edgar Smith had earnestly hoped Denis would
attend, so he could buttonhole him about the story. Later,
Smith did speak to Denis about the matter, urging that, if

---

* Morley still thought so in 1948, the year of "The Man Who
Was Wanted's" long-awaited publication, but the passage of time
had given his view a different twist: "It is odd to recall, thinking
back over past dinners, that one of the pleasantest talks we ever
had was made by Mr. Denis P. S. Conan Doyle. He was naturally
and filially moved by the profound homage implied in our
proceedings. That he afterwards changed his mind, and decided
that in some sinister way the BSI were invading the property rights
of his father's estate, is likely to become a permanent footnote in
literary history."[27]

nothing else, at least a small edition of "The Man Who Was Wanted" be printed for the Baker Street Irregulars. At first, Denis refused, saying that the story was not worthy of his father, but later, according to Smith, he admitted that the Estate wanted to wait until the war was over to publish "The Man Who Was Wanted," so that they could "really cash in" with simultaneous appearances in all the English-speaking countries.[28] *

Whatever else it may have seemed to be, it certainly seemed like good business. It has never been officially disclosed just how much, in fact, the Conan Doyle Estate was eventually paid for the U.S. publication rights to "The Man Who Was Wanted." By November 1942, not very long after the story's existence came to light, Boucher's *San Francisco Chronicle* story reported that two American magazines were already bidding for it, and in October 1943 the London *Evening Standard* reported that an unnamed American magazine had offered the sum of $20,000 for the serial rights, more than had ever been paid before for a short story of its length (approximately 7,000 words).[30] Conan Doyle and Sherlock Holmes were setting records in the literary marketplace once again. But the offers were refused by Adrian, who was reported as still waiting for peacetime to

---

* The BSI continued to petition the Conan Doyle brothers for the release of "The Man Who Was Wanted," even reportedly asking (according to the London *Evening Standard* of October 18, 1943) that the story be cabled to New York at the BSI's expense, to be read to the 1944 BSI annual dinner, all the Irregulars to be sworn to secrecy about it. Edgar Smith's periodic letters to the BSI continued to grumble about the story's being withheld, including a July 1945 comment that Adrian was "still sitting on 'Man Who Was Wanted',," and preparing for publication *The True Conan Doyle,* " 'which' [quoting Adrian] 'will break, once and for all, the parasitical career of that man H. Pearson.' Hot-cha!"[29] ("Hot-cha!" in Smith's original.)

have the story published. Perhaps Adrian and Denis now agreed with Anthony Boucher that "the sixty-first adventure of the master, no matter how inferior to the others, can hardly fail to be the highpoint of any publishing year."[31]

When peace came two years later, however, the story did not leap into print. Or perhaps the periodicals did not leap to buy it. The initial price demanded by the Conan Doyle Estate may have been too high, or perhaps the story, once the avid editors actually had a chance to read it, seemed simply too far below the standard to be accepted. Afterward, it was rumored that the work had made the rounds of all the literary journals in London and that none of them, not even *The Strand Magazine,* would touch it. Whatever the truth, it was not until three years after the war that "The Man Who Was Wanted" finally saw print, six years after its discovery, in the August 1948 issue of the American magazine *Cosmopolitan.* *

> Fierce words, reckless words, imploring words were hurled across the Atlantic at the rock-ribbed Brothers Doyle. Now [exulted Vincent Starrett], we have the story. Some miracle of solicitation turned the trick. Perhaps American dollars had something to do with it.[32] †

The issue was snapped up eagerly by Baker Street Irregulars, who fell upon the story as the materialized answer to their prayers. "FOUND!" exclaimed the magazine's cover: " *The Last Adventure of* SHERLOCK HOLMES, *a hitherto unpublished*

---

* Now retitled "The Case of the Man Who Was Wanted."

†According to Edgar Smith (the late Bliss Austin once recalled), *Cosmopolitan* paid $15,000 for the U.S. publication of "The Man Who Was Wanted." The source of Smith's information is unknown.

story by Sir Arthur Conan Doyle." Five months later, it was published in Great Britain as well, in three installments during the month of January 1949 in London's *Sunday Dispatch.* *

---

* *The Sunday Dispatch* paid only £250 for "The Man Who Was Wanted" — a disappointingly low figure prompting editor Charles Eade to console the Conan Doyle brothers with a promise to seek syndication for the story "throughout the Empire" and to encourage moviemaker Sydney Box to film it.[33] (There was some confusion regarding the payment between the two brothers. Adrian had expected guineas, not pounds; and whereas Denis had instructed that the money be paid into the Estate's London bank account, Adrian had directed the Estate's literary agents, Pearn, Pollinger & Higham, to send the money to him in Turin, Italy.[34])

III

But, once people read "The Man Who Was Wanted," the
overwhelming reaction was quite negative. Even *Cosmopolitan*
had felt a trifle . . . uneasy? At the end of the story was an
editorial note, admitting that there were "several inconsis-
tencies" in the tale, which the magazine had published as
found, except for minor changes in spelling and punctuation.*
The inclination of the Baker Street Irregulars, partly playful,
but increasingly serious, was to treat the story as doubly
apocryphal, the work of neither Dr. John H. Watson nor Sir
Arthur Conan Doyle. Vincent Starrett reported as much in
his *Chicago Tribune* column, and yet he also thought from the
first that the grumbling was a bit unfair:

> It is not a bad story, but one understands why Sir
> Arthur laid it aside. No doubt he intended to
> return to it some day, to give it the extra vitality,
> the special flavor, that would bring it to satisfying
> stature among the other adventures. As it stands,

---

*This note appeared at the end of the final installment in the
Sunday Dispatch as well, along with another note signed by Denis
Conan Doyle: "My father apparently withheld publication of 'The
Case of the Man Who Was Wanted' because he did not consider it
to be up to his usual standard. His family took the same view and
for that reason have withheld publication until now but public
interest in this story has been so great that we have finally yielded
to pressure and decided to allow it to be published in *The Sunday
Dispatch*."

the tale lacks incident and pace; but the idea is ingenious, and there are passages that remind one of some of the best episodes in the saga; in particular the early paragraphs of banter between the detective and Dr. Watson, involving a spot of typical Holmesian deduction.[35]

The Conan Doyle Estate had said from the first that the story was below average, and it had simply turned out to be true. "Speaking for myself," Starrett continued,

> I am happy that the "lost" story had been found and has been published. I should never have ceased to abuse the younger Doyles if they had not released it; and others too, in number, would have upbraided them.[36]

Undoubtedly true, but still the Baker Street Irregulars were not inclined to accept the story as genuine. Edgar W. Smith listed it as a pastiche in his recently founded *Baker Street Journal*, Jay Finley Christ listed it among the Apocrypha in his *Irregular Guide* and *Irregular Chronology*, and more than one Irregular denounced "The Man Who Was Wanted" as a forgery, perhaps a deliberate one.[37] *

---

*Not that this view was universal among Baker Street Irregulars. James C. Iraldi of New York, for example, later wrote Arthur Whitaker to tell him: "Contrary to what other Holmesians may think or say, I am enormously attached to your contribution to the Holmes tales, and can still feel the 'great & glorious feeling' I experienced when reading it for the first time. It is a fact that so much did I think of it that I removed it from its lurid and inane surroundings in order to bind it myself as a separate and priceless unit. It has since become a part of my Sherlock Holmes Collection, and there it shall remain, as honoured and as treasured a tale as any in the famous series."[38]

But the matter was not allowed to rest even there for long. In November 1948, Vincent Starrett received a letter out of the blue from Hesketh Pearson in London. Someone in the United States had sent Pearson a clipping of his September 19 "Books Alive" column discussing the publication, and dubious authorship, of "The Man Who Was Wanted." Could Starrett please let him know in what magazine or newspaper it had appeared, so he could obtain a copy? "Since the publication of my book on Doyle," Pearson wrote, "I have since received information about this story which would interest you and all the Sherlockians in the States; but before imparting it I should like to see the story in print."[39] Starrett, whose curiosity must have been greatly piqued, put a copy of the August *Cosmopolitan* into the mail to him.

Pearson wrote to Starrett again at the beginning of the new year, on January 2, 1949, and the story he imparted was a startling one:

> In September '45, some two years after the appearance of my book on Doyle, I heard from Mr. Arthur Whitaker, a Sheffield architect, who told me that he was the author of the story, which he had written about 35 years before and sent to Doyle suggesting that they collaborate. Mr. Whitaker will give you all the details, and all I need say is that Doyle gave him ten guineas for the right to use the plot in any way he cared. That explains how it came to be among Doyle's papers, and the opening caught the Holmes–Watson manner so well that I believed it to be authentic, though I recognized that the ensuing story fell short of the beginning. I told Mr. Whitaker that in future editions of my book I would correct the error; but it so happened that when Guild Books

did a cheap edition the proofs were not sent to me
and the mistake remained unrectified.[40]

In 1947, Pearson had offered to turn over to the American
expatriate mystery writer John Dickson Carr, then at work
on the research for his *Life of Sir Arthur Conan Doyle,* all the
additional information about Conan Doyle that he had
received after the publication of his own book in 1943. But
Pearson had not received any reply to his letter to Carr, a
silence presumably at the behest of Adrian Conan Doyle,
who was working closely with Carr on this project. Con-
sidering the Estate's attitude toward him, Pearson thought,
"it would be better if I took no hand in the dissemination of
facts concerning this recently published story," and so he
had contacted Whitaker and suggested that he write directly
to Starrett. "Their past attitude shows that they would
regard anything I said as malicious, so I had better keep
right out of it, especially as we do not want Mr. Whitaker's
explanation to be prejudiced by their antagonisms to me."[41]
    Pearson had told Whitaker, in a letter dated September
26, 1945, that he would have the mistake corrected in future
editions of his biography — without any suggestion of alerting
the Conan Doyle family beforehand. Nor did Whitaker
suggest such a thing in his November 3, 1945, reply to
Pearson. In retrospect, one must wonder why alerting the
Conan Doyle family to the mistake that had been made
about the story's authorship did not occur to either of them.
Now that it had been published, keeping right out of the
matter had *not* been Pearson's first thought. "I would like to
tell the truth in an article on the subject for some American
paper," he wrote Whitaker on October 31, 1948, asking for
permission to use his name, and for the loan of Conan
Doyle's 1911 letter to Whitaker for proof. Whitaker told
Pearson on November 2 that he had no objections and that,
while he had been unable to locate Conan Doyle's letter, he

did still have his typescript carbon copy of "The Man Who Was Wanted."

By Christmas, however, Pearson had had second thoughts, as he informed Whitaker on December 27, and now wanted to let Vincent Starrett do it, "which will be of service to him and of enormous interest to the Yankee Holmesians."[42] Or should they just let it drop, Pearson asked Whitaker in a postscript to that letter — or would Whitaker care to take it up himself with Starrett? Perhaps Pearson should not come into it at all, the modest biographer mused. Whitaker agreed on December 31 that Pearson's position was "rather a delicate one," taking the somewhat naïve view that, given the controversy over the story's authenticity, "when the true explanation of its origin is made known, nobody would question it — especially as I should not stand to gain anything by fabricating such a claim."[43] Whitaker thought Pearson's suggestion that he take the matter up himself with Vincent Starrett the best course to follow.

Whitaker wrote to Starrett on January 3 from his home at Stroud, Gloucestershire, setting forth the history of "The Man Who Was Wanted" in detail. In 1910, he had been a young and under-worked architect in Barnsley, Yorkshire, newly married and in need of a little extra money. He was a great admirer of Conan Doyle's Sherlock Holmes stories and had worked out what he thought were a half-dozen good plots. He wrote one out in the best imitation of Conan Doyle's style that he could manage and sent it to the famous author with the suggestion that perhaps they might collaborate. As he told Starrett:

> Instead of getting the snub which I deserved, I received a very kind reply from Doyle in which he said he read my story with interest and liked it; told me that he was getting what was probably a

record price from the Strand Magazine for his
S. H. stories and that any collaboration with an
unknown writer was quite out of the question as,
apart from any other reason, it would reduce his
price by half.[44]

Conan Doyle had recommended that Whitaker try to
publish the story on his own, with characters of his own. But
he also offered to give him ten guineas for it, "on the
understanding that he was at perfect liberty to use, or not
use, the whole or any part of the plot at any future time just
as he thought fit."[45] Whitaker accepted the offer, and Conan
Doyle sent him a check. Whitaker proceeded to write up four
more detective stories, and actually published one in *The
Novel Magazine* before his architectural practice picked up
and absorbed his energies again. It was the end of
Whitaker's career as a writer.

Now that "The Man Who Was Wanted" had been
mistakenly published as by Sir Arthur Conan Doyle,
Whitaker continued, he was concerned that the error be
corrected, in justice to Conan Doyle's memory. On Pearson's
advice, he was disposed to place the problem in Starrett's
hands. For proof of his account, he said, he still had his
carbon copy of the story. Conan Doyle's letter, unfortunately,
had been given away years before and could not be found
now. He expressed his hope that the news of "The Man
Who Was Wanted's" actual authorship would cause no
problem between the Conan Doyle Estate and the publisher
of *Cosmopolitan:*

> The mistake has clearly been a genuine one on the
> part of everybody concerned and entirely due to
> my typescript having been filed away amongst
> Doyle's papers with no attached note as to its
> origin.[46]

Before Starrett could reply, however, a now downcast Whitaker wrote again on January 12, 1949. He had discovered that "The Man Who Was Wanted" was being serialized in the London *Sunday Dispatch* — the first installment had appeared on January 2 — and he felt that he was now compelled to write directly to Denis Conan Doyle, the Trustee of the Estate, and disclose the true authorship of the story, "otherwise he may be involved in no end of trouble later with various publishers."[47]

He wrote to Denis that same day, setting forth the same account of how the tale had come to be written, to be found years later among Sir Arthur's papers. He explained that he had informed Hesketh Pearson of the facts when he read of the story's discovery in Pearson's biography of Conan Doyle, and enclosed a copy of his January 3 letter to Vincent Starrett. He concluded:

> I sincerely hope that you won't have to curse me for involving you in a lot of tiresome correspondence over the business, but feel that you will appreciate that I am not to blame for the unfortunate mistake which has arisen through nobody's fault and that it is causing me a great deal of work and worry also.[48]

There was a great deal more work and worry ahead for Whitaker. Denis Conan Doyle's thoughts are not on record, but Adrian Conan Doyle certainly appreciated no such thing. He was now living in Morocco, a long way away from Inland Revenue, but Denis cabled him immediately about Whitaker's letter and claim. On January 21, Vincent Starrett received a cable from Adrian, from his fastness in Tangier:

> INFORMED A MAN NAMED WHITAKER WRITTEN YOU
> CLAIMING AUTHORSHIP MAN WANTED. KINDLY

UNDERSTAND THAT EXECUTORS MY FATHER'S ESTATE
DENY SUCH CLAIM ABSOLUTELY AS NO SHRED OF
PROOF OR EVIDENCE HAS BEEN PRODUCED. HAVE
INSTRUCTED ATTORNEYS SUE IMMEDIATELY FOR
DAMAGES ANY PERSON CASTING ASPERSIONS UPON
OUR MANUSCRIPT.[49]

Following quickly upon the cable was a letter from Adrian
dated the same day, and it is clear from his remarks that it
was the connection of Hesketh Pearson with the affair which
had inflamed him.

> Dear Mr. Vincent Starrett,
>   Further to my cable, I understand that you
> have received a letter from a man named
> Whitaker, presumably a harmless (?) madman.
> The MS. of Man Who Was Wanted was found
> among some of my father's papers and I have no
> doubt whatever of its authenticity. As a literary
> man, you have had probably some previous
> experience of this kind of thing and the affair could
> have no importance, were it not for the fact that
> this man, instead of writing to the family and
> producing proofs of his most questionable claim,
> wrote instead to that bogus fellow Pearson whose
> fake "Biography" of my father was publicly
> exposed in my book The True Conan Doyle. Now,
> as Dickson Carr's great Biography of my father is
> about to appear, the times must be extremely
> uncomfortable for Pearson, and the whole incident
> smells so strongly of fish that we have put this
> otherwise absurd affair into the hands of our
> lawyers with instructions to demand immediate
> evidence from Whitaker, and in the certain event
> that no such evidence is forthcoming to sue both
> Whitaker and Pearson in the event that either

should circulate falsehoods apropos a manuscript that we have every reason to believe to be perfectly genuine.

As you are an old friend of my father, I just wanted you to know the facts, and I would be very glad if you would ensure that no fabrications result in America. In the event that Whitaker can show one scrap of evidence — as I have privately demanded of him — I will let you know at once. In that event, we would insist on "Cosmopolitan" publishing an explanatory notice and taking back the money that they paid for the original publication. As honourable people, we could do nothing less.

But if, as I believe, Whitaker turns out to be a publicity-seeking fraud, then he and his associate, if any, in England, had better beware.

Kindest regards,

yours sincerely,

ADRIAN M. CONAN DOYLE

Strong words.* Starrett sent back a guarded and neutral reply on February 3, stating his obvious interest in the

---

*But those familiar with Adrian's style when his blood was up will recognize this as just one of many such letters from his pen. Apropos of "Dickson Carr's great Biography" of his father, for example, when Harold Nicolson declared himself unimpressed by Sir Arthur Conan Doyle in a February 4, 1949, review of the book in the *Daily Telegraph,* Adrian called the famous diplomat and man of letters "that rat" and "a renegade socialist of the vilest type" in a February 17, 1949, letter to Denis. Accusing Nicolson of using the book review as "an excuse to personally insult both our father and grandmother," Adrian had sent the offending critic "a challenge to meet me in France and to give me satisfaction with whatever weapons he may choose. . . . Rest assured," he told Denis, "that I

subject, his appreciation at having Adrian's statement on the Estate's position, and his desire to hear the outcome. The affair passed into the hands of each party's attorneys, and for a time silence fell. Whitaker wrote an apologetic note to Starrett on February 10, regretting that he had had to turn away the *Chicago Tribune's* British correspondent, Arthur Veysey, without an interview, and it was clear from his tone that he felt rather under pressure.*

For good reason, as some harsh words were being directed his way, behind the scenes. ("The curious mistake as to authorship has involved me in so much correspondence," Whitaker later wrote to Irregular Nathan Bengis of New York City, "—some of it far from pleasant—that at one time I almost wished I had not attempted to correct it!"[50]) Adrian had written to Whitaker directly on January 21, 1949: "I am amazed and, I must confess, extremely angry with the contents of your letter of January 12th."[51] He demanded tangible proofs of Whitaker's authorship of "The Man Who Was Wanted," and also demanded to know "why did you not write to the family in the first place, instead of writing to the man Pearson whose so-called 'Biography' of my father was a notorious travesty," etc., etc., at some length, closing with the threat of a lawsuit for damages against anyone disparaging the Estate's claim without solid proof. Whitaker's reply of January 28 showed him quite stunned by the Conan Doyle family's reaction:

---

shall do my best to put two feet of steel through this blackguard. If he refuses, then I shall proclaim him a coward at the top of my voice. . . . I will not rest until the insults have been crammed down Nicholson's [*sic*] throat."

*Whitaker turned Veysey away on his solicitor's advice. Veysey did see Whitaker's solicitor, but was told not much more than Vincent Starrett already knew, on the grounds that the delicate matter was being resolved between the parties' legal representatives.

How could I be familiar with the relations between you and Mr. Hesketh Pearson?* I should have expected you to have been the first to blame me had I allowed the story to be wrongfully attributed to your father. Surely you cannot wish such an error to be perpetuated? It never crossed my mind that you would doubt the true facts. Yet your letter seems to imply that I am making a false claim. Surely you can see that such an implication is both unkind and uncalled for? What have I to gain which would induce me to make such a claim if true or not?[52]

Whitaker assured Adrian that he did have solid proof of his authorship, and that "it would be a waste of your time and mine if you did anything so foolish as to bring the action for damages which you suggest."[53]

And it did not take long for the controversy to be resolved. On February 3, 1949, Whitaker was glad to inform his solicitor, J. W. Saleby, that he had succeeded in locating Sir Arthur's 1911 letter to him. (He asked Saleby to make a photostat of it to send to Vincent Starrett, but almost immediately changed his mind, fearing that it would not be "considerate to the present Doyles. American journalists might make too much of the fact that Sir Arthur admits sometimes buying ideas or plots.") Saleby wrote the next day to the Estate's solicitors, Vertue, Son & Churcher, informing them that Whitaker possessed ample proof of his

------

*Actually, he knew now, even if he had not known in 1945: Pearson had told Whitaker about the Conan Doyles' hostility toward him, in his letter of December 27, 1948, and Whitaker had acknowledged the information in his reply of December 31. Yet Whitaker had still taken Pearson's advice to put his story in the hands of Vincent Starrett, an American journalist.

claim, having been actuated throughout by the best motives. A meeting of the solicitors took place in London the week of February 15; the evidence was examined, and the determination was made in favor of Whitaker's claim. All those years, he had kept his carbon copy of the typescript of "The Man Who Was Wanted," and it matched the typescript discovered among Sir Arthur Conan Doyle's papers, down to each error of spelling and punctuation referred to by *Cosmopolitan*. And he had retrieved Conan Doyle's original holograph letter to him from an autograph-collecting relative. Written at Windlesham, Conan Doyle's Sussex home, and dated March 7, 1911, it read:

> Dear Sir,
>
> I read your story. It is not bad and I don't see why you should not change the names, and try to get it published yourself. Of course you could not use the names of my characters.
>
> It is impossible for me to join with another in any case for the result would be that my price would at once be knocked down 75 per cent by Editors.
>
> Sometimes I am open to purchase ideas which I lay aside and use at my own time in my own way. I did this once before and gave 10 guineas for the idea, working it on my own lines. If you wished I would do this for you, but I would not guarantee ever to use it, and you could get no personal credit from it. On the whole you would be wiser to use it yourself.
>
> > Yours faithfully,
> > ARTHUR CONAN DOYLE

"Mr. Whitaker, through his Solicitors," Vertue, Son & Churcher wrote to Starrett at Adrian's request, on February 15, 1949,

expresses that he does not wish to make any
publicity or gain out of the matter, and we most
sincerely hope that the matter can rest there
without unnecessary publicity, as we are quite
confident, and Mr. Whitaker is also confident, that
the mistake made by Sir Arthur's two sons, as to
the authenticity of the manuscript, was made in all
good faith, there being no indication that the
manuscript was not written by Sir Arthur.[54] *

"And so 'The Case of the Man Who Was Wanted' is only a
pastiche, after all!" wrote Starrett in his *Chicago Tribune*
column of March 13, 1949.[56] The story had been broken by
an article by Arthur Veysey in the February 17 issue of that
newspaper,[57] but now Starrett published the details of the
discovery of the true author, minus Hesketh Pearson's role —
not the entire story, but the one for which the world (or at
least the Conan Doyle Estate) was prepared. A more
detailed but still incomplete account appeared in *The Trib,*
the newspaper's house organ.[58] About a month later,
Starrett received a letter from Hesketh Pearson:

I heard obliquely of the Whitaker–Doyle get-
together, but after his announcement to me that he
had written to Denis Doyle I have heard nothing
from Whitaker. I read in the Sunday newspaper

---

* "It would take me pages to go into all the details," Adrian
wrote on February 17, 1949, to Denis in Mysore, India, where he
was tiger-hunting as the guest of a maharajah, "but there is no
question that Whitaker's claim to the authorship is correct. I am
glad to say that the position is quite elucidated by a letter from
Daddy to Whitaker." But Adrian was only partly mollified:
"Whitaker is not out for trouble, but merely wants to rectify a
perfectly natural mistake. The real rascal is that swine Pearson,
who failed to give Whitaker our address."[55]

that published the story that the Doyle estate had given some of the money received for it to Whitaker; but otherwise I know nothing of the proceedings behind the iron Doyle curtain.[59]

Whitaker apparently had concluded that discretion, especially *vis-à-vis* the despised Hesketh Pearson, was one of the Conan Doyle Estate's conditions for a monetary settlement.

The Estate did refund part of the money paid for "The Man Who Was Wanted" to the *Sunday Dispatch,* which turned it over to Whitaker. Or so that newspaper reported on February 27, 1949:

> Mr. Whitaker's wife is seriously ill and temporarily blind, a fact which is naturally a strain on his resources. In these circumstances, the Editor has decided that certain moneys which Mr. Denis Conan Doyle at once suggested should be returned to the *Sunday Dispatch* could appropriately be paid to this author of a story which has provided so much varied interest to the public.[60]

The facts, though, were slightly different. The Estate sent Whitaker's solicitor a check for £150 — sixty percent of the *Sunday Dispatch* payment, a sum rather less than five percent of the reported U.S. payment alone — £21 of which went for the retired architect's legal expenses. Whitaker, a man of very modest means, had hoped that the Conan Doyle Estate would accept responsibility for the expense of setting the matter straight, and Vertue, Son & Churcher on the Estate's behalf had agreed to this, according to J. W. Saleby's memorandum of record for his meeting with Vertue, Son & Churcher — but, in the end, that did not happen. "In the circumstances it has not been possible to make them pay the costs in addition" to the £150 payment, Saleby informed Whitaker on March 25, 1949.[61] Whitaker did not bother to protest. "May I send you my personal and very sincere thanks for your great kindness in dealing so generously with me over the curious case of 'The Man Who Was Wanted'," he wrote to Adrian Conan Doyle on March 30.[62]

Another condition was the avoidance of publicity. The Conan Doyle Estate felt embarrassed (not to mention furious) about the turn of events and obviously wished to hear no more about it. "I am glad to say that the whole absurd affair is now at an end," Adrian wrote to Vincent Starrett on March 29.[63] Whitaker was anxious to comply. For one thing, the Conan Doyle Estate had no wish to see "The Man Who Was Wanted" in print in the future, and Whitaker's solicitor assured the Conan Doyles that Whitaker "naturally quite realizes that he has parted with all ownership in the copyright in the story."[64] For another, "the Doyle solicitors told mine," Whitaker confided to Nathan Bengis on May 31,

> that whilst, of course, they had no objection to my having these [other three detective] stories published they did not wish them to be publicized as having been written by the author of the apocryphal Sherlock Holmes story 'The Man Who Was Wanted' which achieved such notoriety. . . . They have been generous to me and I naturally wish to do nothing to which they would take exception.[65]

Still, Whitaker needed the money that he might be paid for these stories, if he could get them published. It had been on his mind from the first: on the same day he first wrote to Vincent Starrett — January 3, 1949 — Whitaker had written a second letter to him, a sort of afterthought that raised the possibility of *Cosmopolitan* publishing his other old stories on the strength of the publicity that would result when the true authorship of "The Man Who Was Wanted" was revealed. Whitaker's wife was recuperating slowly from her illness, and Whitaker himself was sixty-six years old and not in good health. He evidently thought that the flurry over the authorship of "The Man Who Was Wanted" had created the opportunity to sell these decades-old stories. He did not think, he told Bengis, that the Conan Doyle Estate would object to a simple statement that the stories were by the author of "The Man Who Was Wanted." Bengis took the trouble to write to several American magazines on Whitaker's behalf, but without success in the short time before he received a letter from Whitaker's son-in-law, informing him that Arthur Whitaker had died suddenly in July 1949.[66]

IV

So that is how the true authorship of "The Man Who Was Wanted" came to light and was determined. Some final considerations remain.

One is concerned with what was done to rectify the error that had been published. The *Sunday Dispatch* did run its news story of February 27, 1949,[67] revealing that "The Man Who Was Wanted" had turned out to be not the work of Sir Arthur Conan Doyle.* But, rather contrary to the ethics of publishing and journalism, *Cosmopolitan* never did. Despite Adrian's assurance to Vincent Starrett that the Estate would insist upon *Cosmopolitan* publishing a retraction, in the event that Whitaker's claim turned out to be true, none ever appeared. Letters from Baker Street Irregulars to the editor of *Cosmopolitan,* then and later, asking for clarification, went unprinted and unanswered. Whether any of the money paid by *Cosmopolitan* for "The Man Who Was Wanted" was returned to it by the Conan Doyle Estate is unknown. There is just a brief note from Whitaker's solicitor to his client, dated February 26, 1949, warning that "Mr. Churcher thinks you should not discuss this matter with the press, particularly with The Associated Press of America, as matters have not yet been finally fixed with 'The Cosmopolitan'."[68] Saleby repeated this advice to Whitaker a

---

*Whitaker's solicitor had been able to "peruse and finally approve" this article before publication, according to the final bill for his services.

month later: "You may think me ultra-fussy, but I do not want you involved in any further trouble."[69]

In any event, it was not until 1963 that the Conan Doyle Estate, in the form of a letter from Adrian, directly acknowledged the original error. Discussion about "The Man Who Was Wanted" in the pages of *The Sherlock Holmes Journal* revealed that there were still people in Great Britain, even Holmesians, members of the Sherlock Holmes Society of London, who were unaware of the mistake that had been made years before about the story's authorship. Adrian, now domiciled in baronial splendor at the Château de Lucens near Geneva, Switzerland, responded to the questioning with a letter to the editor which included a snarl at the "childish and stupid joke" of referring to Sir Arthur Conan Doyle as Dr. Watson's "literary agent" and elaborately denying his authorship of the Holmesian Canon.[70] (A BSI conceit for which Adrian had no patience: "The Holmes Cult in America is offensive to the last degree," he once wrote to the president of the Sherlock Holmes Society of London, S. C. Roberts, "and, as far as the alleged experts are concerned, may be fairly divided between those who use Sherlock Holmes as a means of publicity for themselves and those who have worked themselves into such a state of hysteria that they really hate my father for creating something that never actually lived."[71])

Another consideration is just how the tale came to be preserved and consequently discovered later. Some ten years after the story's publication, Adrian told the prolific English writer Michael Harrison, who had just published his instant classic *In the Footsteps of Sherlock Holmes* (1958), "what really happened" in the case of "The Man Who Was Wanted." His father, said Adrian, never got his plots from other people, and, when Sir Arthur received Whitaker's letter with the enclosed Sherlock Holmes story, he simply crumpled them up and threw them into the wastepaper basket, philanthropically offering Whitaker ten guineas. But Lady

Conan Doyle always went through the wastepaper baskets before the servants were allowed to empty them. She "rescued" every scrap of paper, carefully laying them up against . . . who could tell? And that, according to Adrian, was how "The Man Who Was Wanted," which Lady Conan Doyle took to be her husband's work, came to be among Sir Arthur's papers thirty years later.[72]

Just how Adrian could be so sure in this particular case is unclear, since both his parents had been dead for some years prior to the story's discovery. Nor does Adrian's explanation hold up well against Conan Doyle's own letter to Whitaker. In it, Sir Arthur said, straightforwardly and without blushing, that he had once before bought and used an idea for a story from someone else; and he was offering to do it again, though he might not (and in fact did not) ever use this one. There is a telling inconsistency in this version of Adrian's tale, also: Whitaker's letters should also have been in that wastepaper basket sometime, for Lady Conan Doyle to find and read—but seemingly they were not?

It is not that Adrian's tale is impossible. It *is* possible; only it contradicts Sir Arthur Conan Doyle, a man whose honor Adrian would not wish us to question or challenge. Why would he prefer this tale to his father's own letter to Arthur Whitaker? Because, it seems, Adrian was particularly sensitive and defensive about the notion of his father buying an idea or plot for a story—apparently feeling that Sir Arthur might be lessened as a writer in the eyes of others. To the end of his life, Adrian denied what his father had acknowledged in his 1911 letter to Whitaker. Had he forgotten that he had sent a copy of that letter to Vincent Starrett in 1949? It seems so. "Though he had every right to buy a suggestion for a mere plot, which is a common practise [*sic*] among authors," he told William S. Baring-Gould in a long letter dated January 20, 1966, reviewing the draft introductory chapters for *The Annotated Sherlock Holmes*—and instructing him to alter his discussion of "The Man Who

Was Wanted"—"Conan Doyle did not use other men's writings, whether superior or inferior."[73]

To more than one observer, on the other hand, it was Adrian's tale which fell rather short of flattering his father, in making him crumple up and throw away a story sent to him. Most people receive matter of one sort or another for which they have no use, but it would not be the act of a gentleman to throw something of this sort away, instead of returning it courteously. And Sir Arthur Conan Doyle was a courteous gentleman if he was anything at all. But Adrian wanted to pass it all off as an act of charity on his father's part, a putative aspect that he called "the only important part of this affair."[74]

Adrian's persistent attempts to avoid the facts that he found unpleasant about "The Man Who Was Wanted," first its actual authorship and then how it had come to be among his father's papers, led many to wonder whether he had attempted to perpetrate an outright fraud. Did Adrian recognize "The Man Who Was Wanted" as an imitation by some unknown hand but decide to risk exploiting it commercially as Sir Arthur Conan Doyle's work nonetheless? A different way to pose this question is to ask whether there were some way in which Adrian should have been able to recognize "The Man Who Was Wanted" as an imitation.

The specific point about "The Man Who Was Wanted" that aroused the suspicions of many Baker Street Irregulars in regard to Adrian's probity in the matter is the fact that it was a typescript which had been discovered. Adrian seems always to have referred to it as a manuscript, and in fact the original Associated Press dispatch by William King, of September 12, 1942, actually stated that "it is in the same neat handwriting which characterized all his manuscripts."*

---

* This passage may have been based upon a remark of Adrian's which appeared in the original London *Star* report of June 13,

Mysteriously, this one sentence was dropped from the published version of the dispatch which appeared the next day in the *New York Times,* the only textual change of any significance. Presumably, it was not AP news editor Charles Honce who deleted it, for the sentence appears in two later reprintings of the dispatch in Sherlockian works by Honce.[75] It seems unlikely that anyone at the *New York Times* could have read that sentence in the AP dispatch and deleted it because he knew better; but in fact the discovered story was *not* holograph, and thus properly not a manuscript at all. It was not until the *Sunday Dispatch's* article of February 27, 1949, however, that the public was first informed that "The Man Who Was Wanted" had been a typescript.[76] And the attention of some Baker Street Irregulars was instantly riveted upon that fact, because there is no doubt that Sir Arthur Conan Doyle never used a typewriter; Adrian himself was on record on that point. But, in justice to Adrian, while it is true that typescripts of Sir Arthur's stories may have been unusual in his house, still they were not unknown. Occasionally, Conan Doyle did send manuscripts out to be typed and returned to him for revision.[77]

Other suspicions were aroused by the style of the story and its weakness of plot. But it should be remembered that, if "The Man Who Was Wanted" were feeble, so were "The Veiled Lodger," "The Yellow Face," and one or two other Sherlock Holmes adventures indubitably from Sir Arthur's pen. Lady Conan Doyle believed "The Man Who Was Wanted" to be genuine, innocently enough, while years later

---

1942: "Every line of my father's stories, from the earliest days, was in his own neat writing." While the *Star* story did not specifically link this remark to "The Man Who Was Wanted" as discovered among Sir Arthur's papers, it certainly gave readers the impression that it was a holograph manuscript that had been found.

her daughter Jean, finding herself unexpectedly reading it for the first time in the *Sunday Dispatch,* did not. She was certain that it was not her father's work, she had been told nothing of its impending publication, and she was a bit put out with her brother Adrian.[78] He himself realized that the story was not up to the standard but evidently believed "The Man Who Was Wanted" to be his father's work nonetheless. He saw no reason to assume that a Sherlock Holmes story found among his father's papers would be anything other than just that. Vincent Starrett felt that no fraud was involved, that the episode had arisen simply from Adrian's cupidous desire to believe, combined with a lack of sensitivity on his part—that Adrian "lacked the special knowledge, or insight, or prescience (or whatever it is) of dyed-in-the-wool enthusiasts like ourselves, for whom the story did not 'ring true'."[79] Some have that sensitivity, while others do not. Only one of Conan Doyle's children had it, and she had not been consulted.

But, even though there had been no fraud, Starrett did think that the entire affair could have been handled with more intelligence by everyone concerned. This included Arthur Whitaker. What was his motive in raising the question of the authorship of "The Man Who Was Wanted"? Perhaps he did believe that justice to Conan Doyle's memory called for the error to be corrected. But there is no doubt also that Whitaker saw profit and publicity for himself in the situation. This is manifest in that second of two letters which Whitaker wrote to Vincent Starrett on January 3, 1949, when the ink was scarcely dry on the first:

> I have just wondered whether it might be worthwhile asking [the editor of *Cosmopolitan*] whether he would consider the possibility of publishing one or more of the three detective stories I wrote at the same time as "The Man Who Was Wanted" and

which never have been published? This he might feel inclined to do partly on the strength of the undeserved notoriety I have achieved by my plagiarism having been at least good enough to cause some unexpected and quite unintentional deception in literary circles! If you thought it might be worth submitting the tales to him I would do so.[80]

Whitaker did succeed in obtaining some profit and publicity from the situation, though not nearly as smoothly as he had expected, and his other three detective stories never did see print.

"I find it difficult to be sentimental about Whitaker," Starrett wrote a decade after the affair, "and it may be that my dislike of him has colored some of my thinking."[81] Contemplating the misadventure, Starrett had been forced to wish aloud that Whitaker had hugged his secret to his bosom and maintained a golden silence. He wrote in his *Chicago Tribune* column of March 13, 1949:

I do not question his distress in this connection, but I wonder how much he has really improved the situation for Conan Doyle by his tardy revelation of authorship. . . . I don't insist on this—I may be altogether wrong—but I think the argument has merit.[82]

But in retrospect, it is, for once, impossible to agree with Starrett.

And even if Whitaker had remained silent in 1949, would Hesketh Pearson have done likewise? Possibly. He knew the truth when "The Man Who Was Wanted" was published; at least he knew of Whitaker's claim; but he lacked the documentary evidence—the typescript's carbon copy, Conan Doyle's 1911 letter to Whitaker — to prove the claim, had he wished to press it. Certainly he had had provocation enough in the past to make the idea of making Adrian uncomfortable a very tempting one. Not only had Adrian turned on him in 1944, but in 1947 he had also (unsuccessfully) tried to prevent the British Publishers Guild from issuing a new edition of *Conan Doyle: His Life and Art* by misinforming the Guild's officials that the Estate intended to sue Pearson for criminal libel.[83] One can detect a certain slyness in the way that Pearson dealt with the issue of "The Man Who Was Wanted," and perhaps these affronts were on Pearson's mind when he advised Arthur Whitaker to write to Vincent Starrett.

Years later, in his posthumously published autobiography, Pearson dealt only briefly and humorously with all the trouble he had had over his biography of Sir Arthur Conan Doyle:

> I gather that its frankness did not make all the members of the Doyle family skip for joy, but no honest biographer can hope to please everyone, and it happened that I received a wraithlike commendation of the work. As a rule I dream of my characters while writing about them and occasionally remember scraps of conversation with them after waking up. But I dreamt of Doyle some months after two editions of the biography had sold out. He seemed pleased that I had done him justice, telling me to take no notice of hostile criticism; and as I always act in accordance with dreams when they echo my own feelings, I have followed his advice.[84]

But Adrian's rancor never diminished, and he pursued Pearson the writer's entire life, and even afterward. In 1959,

Sir Arthur Conan Doyle's centenary, Adrian prevented Pearson from giving a BBC Radio talk about his father. The choice given the BBC was either to cancel Pearson's broadcast or to forego the use of any of Sir Arthur's works for the remainder of the period protected by British copyright, through 1980. Pearson understood the BBC's predicament and consented to his broadcast's cancellation.[85] Later, in 1962, when the San Francisco Public Library mounted an exhibit honoring the 75th anniversary of *A Study in Scarlet,* Adrian wrote demanding that Pearson's biography be removed from display, accusing him of criminal libel there and elsewhere. (The library did not accommodate him.) And, in 1966, two years after Pearson's death, Adrian insisted that William S. Baring-Gould remove discussions of Pearson's biography from *The Annotated Sherlock Holmes,* proclaiming that "in the interest of truth I cannot agree to the use of any of my father's writings in any book wherein this charlatan is quoted as a serious authority."[86] And no doubt other instances as well could be found of Adrian's lasting displeasure with Hesketh Pearson.

The pity of it all was that Hesketh Pearson in his own way was truly devoted to Sir Arthur Conan Doyle, whom he had reportedly met as a child, and to Sherlock Holmes. "The first stories I ever read with pleasure were those about Sherlock Holmes," Pearson recalled in his autobiography, "who for me was a real figure, not a figment of the fancy."[87] He had decided to write a biography of Conan Doyle because, "having expressed myself on two heroes of my manhood, Shakespeare and Shaw, I felt like doing the same for a hero of my youth."[88] And, when it came to the misadventure of "The Man Who Was Wanted," it was Adrian who suffered from the feud. Back on January 29, 1942, he had written to Pearson: "I know that you will write this book as you yourself see the facts, unswayed by any but your own powers of perception and reason, and I neither expect nor desire anything more fair than that."[89] Had

Adrian remained constant to that, despite the very real flaws
and shortcomings of Pearson's biography,* had Adrian not
turned on Pearson in 1944, he would probably have been
informed of the story's actual authorship in 1945, when
Pearson first heard from Whitaker. He would have learned
about it privately, quietly, long before any publication, and
so would have been spared considerable embarrassment and
inconvenience later.

But Adrian could not see it that way. To him, Pearson
was "that bogus fellow," and worse, "a professional liar,"[90]
a malicious purveyor of falsehoods and disparagements
against Adrian's revered father. And it was Arthur Whitaker
who was to blame for the trouble that Adrian had had over
"The Man Who Was Wanted," certainly not Adrian himself,
no, not in the least. As Adrian asked Vincent Starrett, quite
rhetorically, in a letter of March 1949:

> Is it not infuriating that one can be put to so much
> trouble and inconvenience, after 40 years, thanks
> directly to the abominable habit of a would-be
> writer in making use of the characters invented by
> an established Author.[91]

"The Man Who Was Wanted" was something of a
milestone in the development of the Conan Doyle Estate's
hostile attitude toward Sherlock Holmes pastiches and those
who wrote them (except, of course, when Adrian decided to
write some himself a few years later).[92] The Estate's attitude
had never been generous, of course; and Adrian Conan
Doyle no doubt felt himself like the poor little Dutch boy

---

* See Jon L. Lellenberg, ed., *The Quest for Sir Arthur Conan Doyle:
Thirteen Biographers in Search of a Life* (Southern Illinois University
Press, 1987) for critiques of this and other biographies of Sir
Arthur Conan Doyle mentioned in this book.

trying to plug up all the holes in the dike, to keep out a rising tide of vile imitations of his father's stories. When he had learned that Ellery Queen had unwittingly reprinted more passages from Sherlock Holmes stories than he had obtained permission for, in his anthology *101 Years' Entertainment: The Great Detective Stories* (1941), Adrian used the inadvertent copyright infringement to force Queen to withdraw his 1944 anthology of Sherlockian parodies and pastiches, *The Misadventures of Sherlock Holmes,* from circulation.[93] And a promising series of Holmes pastiches by mystery writer Stuart Palmer was nipped in the bud after only two stories in 1944, when "the legal heirs of the late Sir Arthur Conan Doyle set up shrill wails of agony at the very idea of the continuance of the series."[94]

But if anything more were needed to convince the irascible Adrian Conan Doyle that pastiches were an outrage, and their writers contemptible scoundrels, it was his experience of Arthur Whitaker's "The Man Who Was Wanted." Adrian clung fiercely to this attitude to the day he died, in June 1970—long past Whitaker's death in 1949, or his brother Denis's in 1955, or even Hesketh Pearson's in 1964—and the effects of his attitude toward imitation Sherlock Holmes adventures by others are still felt today.

Notes

1. Hesketh Pearson, *Conan Doyle: His Life and Art* (London: Methuen, 1943), p. 100. Pearson had already previewed this and a few other Conan Doyle discoveries in an article entitled "Sherlock Holmes and 'The Strand'" in the August 1943 issue of *The Strand Magazine*.

2. Quoted in Ian Hunter, *Nothing to Repent: The Life of Hesketh Pearson* (London: Hamish Hamilton, 1985), p. 182.

3. *Ibid.*

4. Michael Holroyd, "Hesketh Pearson: Biography with Warts," *Confrontation* (Long Island University), No. 15 (Fall 1977/ Winter 1978), pp. 17–24.

5. Letter, Adrian Conan Doyle to Hesketh Pearson, September 24, 1943.

6. Letter, Adrian Conan Doyle to Hesketh Pearson, October 6, 1943.

7. Letter, Adrian Conan Doyle to Hesketh Pearson, November 9, 1943.

8. Letter, Adrian Conan Doyle to Hesketh Pearson, February 20, 1944.

9. Letter, Hesketh Pearson to George Bernard Shaw, February 27, 1944.

10. Letter, George Bernard Shaw to Hesketh Pearson, February 28, 1944.

11. Letter, Pearson to Shaw (February 27, 1944).

12. Letter, Denis Conan Doyle to Hesketh Pearson, March 24, 1945.

13. Holroyd, p. 22.

14. Adrian Conan Doyle, *The True Conan Doyle* (London: John Murray, 1945), p. 5.

15. Hunter, p. 184.

16. Letter, James Agate to Adrian Conan Doyle, October 27, 1945.

17. Letter, James Agate (secretary) to Hesketh Pearson, November 13, 1945.

18. C. B., "Conan Doyle," *Truth,* December 28, 1945.

19. "Star Man's Diary," *Star* (London), June 13, 1942.

20. Edgar W. Smith, *A Baker Street Four-Wheeler* (Maplewood, N.J.: Pamphlet House, 1944), p. 11.

21. Edgar W. Smith, letter, *Saturday Review of Literature,* October 10, 1942.

22. Quoted in Edgar W. Smith, "To the Members of the Baker Street Irregulars" (letter), August 14, 1942 — including the additional cry: "Can't the Irregulars *do* something?"

23. Smith, *ibid.*; Vincent Starrett, "Books Alive," *Chicago Tribune,* September 13, 1942; Anthony Boucher, "The Case of the Sixty-First Adventure," *San Francisco Chronicle,* November 29, 1942.

24. "Conan Doyle Find Stirs Holmes Fans," *New York Times,* September 13, 1942.

25. Letter, Adrian Conan Doyle to Hesketh Pearson, September 11, 1942.

26. Christopher Morley, four-page, typed memoir of the origins of the Baker Street Irregulars, written April 14, 1941, for Old Irregular Henry Morton Robinson.

27. Christopher Morley, "A Note on the Baker Street Irregulars," in the BSI edition of *The Adventure of the Blue Carbuncle* (New York: The Baker Street Irregulars, Inc., 1948), pp. 69–70.

28. Letter, Edgar W. Smith to S. Tupper Bigelow, May 29, 1959.

29. Edgar W. Smith, "To the Members of the Baker Street Irregulars" (letter), July 18, 1945.

30. "£5000 for Story," *Evening Standard* (London), October 18, 1943.

31. Boucher.

32. Vincent Starrett, "Books Alive," *Chicago Tribune,* August 15, 1948.

33. Letter, Charles Eade to Denis Conan Doyle, December 9, 1948.

34. Letter, Nancy Pearn to Denis Conan Doyle, December 17, 1948.

35. Starrett, "Books Alive," August 15, 1948.

36. Vincent Starrett, "Books Alive," *Chicago Tribune,* September 19, 1948.

37. Edgar W. Smith, "Bibliographic Notes," *The Baker Street Journal,* Vol. 3, No. 4 (OLD SERIES) (October 1948), pp. 509–10; Jay Finley Christ, "Second Supplement" to *An Irregular Guide to Sherlock Holmes of Baker Street* and "A Chronological Supplement" to *An Irregular Chronology of Sherlock Holmes of Baker Street* (Chicago: Fanlight House, 1948); and Edgar W. Smith, "From the Editor's Commonplace Book," *The Baker Street Journal* (October 1948), pp. 458–62. Vincent Starrett's September 19, 1948, *Chicago Tribune* column named several other Baker Street Irregulars who refused to believe that Sir Arthur Conan Doyle had been the author of "The Man Who Was Wanted": H. B. Williams of Indianapolis; Joseph Henry Jackson of San Francisco; Russell McLauchlin of Detroit; and Jeremiah Buckley of Chicago.

38. Letter, James C. Iraldi to Arthur Whitaker, May 3, 1949.

39. Letter, Hesketh Pearson to Vincent Starrett, November 8, 1948.

40. Letter, Hesketh Pearson to Vincent Starrett, January 2, 1949.

41. *Ibid.*

42. Letter, Hesketh Pearson to Arthur Whitaker, December 27, 1948.

43. Letter, Arthur Whitaker to Hesketh Pearson, December 31, 1948.

44. Letter, Arthur Whitaker to Vincent Starrett, January 3, 1949.

45. *Ibid.*

46. *Ibid.*

47. Letter, Arthur Whitaker to Vincent Starrett, January 12, 1949.

48. Letter, Arthur Whitaker to Denis Conan Doyle, January 12, 1949.

49. Cablegram, Adrian Conan Doyle to Vincent Starrett, January 21, 1949.

50. Letter, Arthur Whitaker to Nathan Bengis, April 4, 1949.

51. Letter, Adrian Conan Doyle to Arthur Whitaker, January 21, 1949.

52. Letter, Arthur Whitaker to Adrian Conan Doyle, January 28, 1949.

53. *Ibid.*

54. Letter, Vertue, Son & Churcher to Vincent Starrett, February 15, 1949.

55. Letter, Adrian Conan Doyle to Denis Conan Doyle, February 17, 1949.

56. Vincent Starrett, "Books Alive," *Chicago Tribune,* March 13, 1949.

57. "Real Author Solves Doyle Mystery Elementary Way," *Chicago Tribune,* February 17, 1949.

58. "The Case of the Missing Manuscript," *The Trib,* March 1949.

59. Letter, Hesketh Pearson to Vincent Starrett, April 26, 1949.

60. John Bingham, "The Great Sherlock Holmes Mystery," *The Sunday Dispatch,* February 27, 1949.

61. Letter, J. W. Saleby to Arthur Whitaker, March 25, 1949.

62. Letter, Arthur Whitaker to Adrian Conan Doyle, March 30, 1949.

63. Letter, Adrian Conan Doyle to Vincent Starrett, March 29, 1949.

64. Letter, Lapage Norris Sons & Saleby to Vertue, Son & Churcher, February 23, 1949.

65. Letter, Arthur Whitaker to Nathan Bengis, May 31, 1949.

66. Letter, Hugh Dent to Nathan Bengis, July 13, 1949. Whitaker had died on July 10, 1949. See his obituary (which does not mention "The Man Who Was Wanted"): "Natural History Authority," *Stroud News,* July 15, 1949. Whitaker had been an amateur ornithologist of some note.

67. Bingham.

68. Letter, J. W. Saleby to Arthur Whitaker, February 26, 1949.

69. Letter, J. W. Saleby to Arthur Whitaker, March 28, 1949.

70. Adrian Conan Doyle, "Deep Waters" (letter), *The Sherlock Holmes Journal,* Vol. 6, No. 3 (Winter 1963), p. 96.

71. Letter, Adrian Conan Doyle to S. C. Roberts, November 30, 1953.

72. Letter, Adrian Conan Doyle to Michael Harrison, December 6, 1958.

73. Letter, Adrian Conan Doyle to William S. Baring-Gould, January 20, 1966.

74. Adrian Conan Doyle, "Deep Waters."

75. Charles Honce, *Sherlock Holmes Is Still In the News* (Mount Vernon, N.Y.: Golden Eagle Press, January 7, 1944 — distributed at the 1944 BSI annual dinner), reprinted in *Profile by Gaslight* edited by Edgar W. Smith (New York: Simon & Schuster, 1944), pp. 81–84, and *The Public Papers of a Bibliomaniac* (Mount Vernon, N.Y.: Golden Eagle Press, 1942), pp. 159–64.

76. Bingham.

77. See Bliss Austin, "On the Writing of Some of the Most Remarkable Books Ever Penned," *Baker Street Miscellanea*, No. 14 (June 1978), pp. 1–2.

78. Dame Jean Conan Doyle, interview with the author, December 1, 1977. Jean Conan Doyle was serving in the Royal Air Force throughout the period of "The Man Who Was Wanted's" discovery, and afterward, and was stationed in Germany at the time of its publication in 1948 and 1949.

79. Letter, Vincent Starrett to S. Tupper Bigelow, July 16, 1959.

80. Letter, Arthur Whitaker to Vincent Starrett, January 3, 1949 (second letter of that date).

81. Letter, Starrett to Bigelow (July 16, 1959).

82. Starrett, "Books Alive," March 13, 1949.

83. Letter, Alan White (Managing Director of Methuen & Co.) to Hesketh Pearson, February 20, 1949.

84. *Hesketh Pearson By Himself* (New York: Harper & Row, 1966), p. 294.

85. Letter, Vertue, Son & Churcher to Hesketh Pearson, April 3, 1959, and Letter, John Green (BBC Radio) to Hesketh Pearson, April 6, 1959. A shorter version of the script was published by Pearson under the title "More Than Sherlock Holmes" in *The Sunday Times,* May 17, 1959.

86. Letter, Adrian Conan Doyle to Baring-Gould (January 20, 1966).

87. *Hesketh Pearson By Himself,* p. 18.

88. *Ibid.,* p. 293.

89. Letter, Adrian Conan Doyle to Hesketh Pearson, January 29, 1942.

90. Among the many epithets Adrian employed to vilify Hesketh Pearson over the years, these appeared, respectively, in Adrian's letter to Starrett (January 21, 1949) and in his handwritten marginalia on a draft of William S. Baring-Gould's annotations for *The Annotated Sherlock Holmes,* accompanying Adrian's letter to Baring-Gould (January 20, 1966).

91. Letter, Adrian Conan Doyle to Vincent Starrett, March 29, 1949.

92. Adrian Conan Doyle and John Dickson Carr, *The Exploits of Sherlock Holmes* (New York: Random House, 1954). These twelve stories originally appeared in *Life* and *Collier's* in 1952 and 1953.

93. See Francis M. Nevins, Jr., *Royal Bloodline: Ellery Queen, Author and Detective* (Bowling Green, Ohio: Bowling Green State University Popular Press, 1974), pp. 103, 221.

94. Stuart Palmer, "The I.O.U. of Hildegarde Withers," *The Baker Street Journal,* Vol. 3, No. 1 (OLD SERIES) (January 1948), p. 10. The first of Palmer's two pastiches appeared in *Ellery Queen's Mystery Magazine* (July 1944) and the second in the suppressed *Misadventures of Sherlock Holmes.*

Selected Bibliography

BARZUN, JACQUES. "The Other Decalogue." In *Beyond Baker Street: A Sherlockian Anthology* ed. Michael Harrison (Indianapolis: Bobbs-Merrill, 1976), pp. 21–31. An attack upon Sherlock Holmes pastiches, using "The Man Who Was Wanted" to show, incorrectly, that its lack of verisimilitude was due to its having been written in the 1920s by an American journalist colleague of Vincent Starrett's. The record was set straight by Jon L. Lellenberg's letter to the editor of *The Baker Street Journal,* Vol. 28, No. 2 (NS), June 1978, pp. 105–6.

CARR, JOHN DICKSON. *The Life of Sir Arthur Conan Doyle.* New York: Harper, 1949 [pp. 277–78, 291]. The Conan Doyle Estate's version of the story's authorship and suppression, written before the decision to allow its publication, but appearing shortly afterward, and immediately before the discovery of its true authorship.

FLEISSNER, ROBERT F. "The Case *For* 'The Man Who Was Wanted'." *The Sherlock Holmes Journal,* Vol. 19, No. 2, Summer 1989, pp. 50–51. A modern argument estimating its quality higher than most other critics have done, and contending that Arthur Conan Doyle probably planned to make some use of it eventually.

GREEN, RICHARD LANCELYN, ed. *The Further Adventures of Sherlock Holmes.* London: Penguin Books, 1985 [pp. 13–19]. Historical commentary accompanying the story's first British reprinting since 1949, as "The Adventure of the Sheffield Banker."

HAINING, PETER, ed. *The Final Adventures of Sherlock Holmes.* Secaucus, N.J.: Castle Books, 1981 [pp. 18–19]. A weak attempt to ascribe the story's authorship at least partially to Arthur Conan Doyle, in order to justify its inclusion in Haining's collection of Holmesian apocrypha. A more sincere mistaken belief in Conan Doyle's authorship is that of Trevor Hall in *Sherlock Holmes and His Creator* (London: Duckworth, 1978), pp. 136–37.

HONCE, CHARLES. "Sherlock Holmes in the News." In *Profile by Gaslight* ed. Edgar W. Smith (New York: Simon and Schuster, 1944), pp. 81–84. A contemporary account of the story's discovery by a Baker Street Irregular and Associated Press news editor who helped spread the word and arouse a demand to have it published.

PEARSON, HESKETH. *Conan Doyle: His Life and Art.* London: Methuen, 1943 [pp. 98–100]. The original account of the story's discovery, in the biography which infuriated its subject's sons. For an objective critique of this biography, see Nicholas Utechin, "A Good-Natured Debunking," in *The Quest for Sir Arthur Conan Doyle* ed. Jon L. Lellenberg (Carbondale, Ill.: Southern Illinois University Press, 1987), pp. 96–104.

SMITH, EDGAR W. "Introduction" to *The Return of Solar Pons* by August Derleth (Sauk City, Wis.: Mycroft & Moran, 1958), pp. ix–xi. A retrospective discussion of the case by the chairman of the Baker Street Irregulars, who had disbelieved the story's purported Doylean authorship immediately upon its publication in 1948.

TRACY, JACK, ed. *Sherlock Holmes: The Published Apocrypha.* Boston: Houghton Mifflin, 1980 [pp. 299–301]. A historical account of the story's discovery and true authorship, accompanying its first public American printing since 1948. (A small edition had been privately printed and distributed in 1966 by Baker Street Irregular Robert H. Schutz of Pittsburgh, Pa.)

INDEX

Jon L. Lellenberg is "Rodger Prescott of evil memory" in the Baker Street Irregulars, a holder of the BSI's Two Shilling Award, and a charter member of the Arthur Conan Doyle Society. For the past fifteen years, he has served as Contributing Editor of the quarterly journal of Sherlockiana and Doyleana, *Baker Street Miscellanea.* His previous book, *The Quest for Sir Arthur Conan Doyle,* was published by Southern Illinois University Press in 1987. He lives in the Alexandria, Virginia environs of Washington, D.C., where he is clandestinely active in a BSI scion society called "The Bruce-Partington Planners within the Military-Industrial Complex."